# T R E E
## Identification Record Book

Hello Nature

# Your Feedback is Appreciated!!!

Please consider leaving us "5 Stars" on your
Amazon review.

Thank you!

Copyright © 2022 Hello Nature

Published by Hello Nature

This Tree Identification Record Book

Belongs To:

_____

## Environment

Location / GPS: _____  Date _____

Season:  ○ Spring  ○ Summer  ○ Fall  ○ Winter

Surroundings:  ○ Hedgerows  ○ Field  ○ Park  ○ Woodland  ○ Water
○ Other _____

Setting:  ○ Natural  ○ Artificial  **Type:** ○ Evergreen  ○ Deciduous

Notes: _____
_____

## General

Shape:  ○ Vase  ○ Columnar  ○ Round  ○ (Other) _____

Features:  ○ Conical/Spire  ○ Spreading  ○ Upright  ○ Weeping
○ (Other) _____

Branching:  ○ Opposite  ○ Alternate  **Estimated Age:** _____

Notes: _____
_____

## Needles or Leaves

Type:  ○ Needle  ○ Simple Broadleaf  ○ Compound Broadleaf  ○ Scales

Shape:  ○ Cordate (heart-shaped)  ○ Lanceolate (long and narrow)
○ Deltoid (triangular)  ○ Obicular (round)  ○ Ovate (egg-shaped)
○ Palm and Maple  ○ Lobed

Structure:  ○ Simple (attached to twigs or twig stems)
○ Compound (attached to single lead steam)

Notes: _____
_____

## Flowers, Fruits & Seeds

Flower Type:  ○ Single Blooms  ○ Clustered Blooms  ○ Catkins

Fruits / Seeds:  ○ Berries  ○ Apples  ○ Pears  ○ Nuts  ○ Acorns
○ Cones  ○ Capsules  ○ Catkins  ○ (Other) _____

Notes: _____
_____

## Leaf Buds & Twigs

Bud Type:  ○ Terminal (grows at tip of a shoot causing shoot to grow longer)
○ Lateral (grow along sides of a shoot causing sideways growth)

Twig Features:  ○ Smooth  ○ Hairy  ○ Spines  ○ Corky Ribs
○ (Other) _____

Notes: _____

## Bark

Texture:  ○ Furrowed  ○ Scaly  ○ Peeling  ○ Smooth  ○ Shiny
○ Fissured  ○ Ridges / Depressions  ○ Papery  ○ Warty
○ (Other) _____

Color:  ○ Gray  ○ Brown  ○ Cinnamon  ○ While  ○ Silver
○ Green  ○ Copper  ○ (Other) _____

Notes: _____

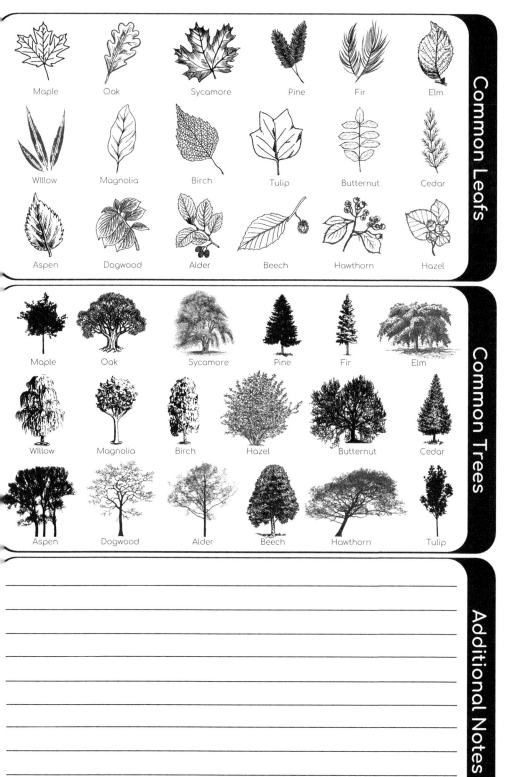

Maple
Oak
Sycamore
Pine
Fir
Elm

Willow
Magnolia
Birch
Tulip
Butternut
Cedar

Aspen
Dogwood
Alder
Beech
Hawthorn
Hazel

Maple
Oak
Sycamore
Pine
Fir
Elm

Willow
Magnolia
Birch
Hazel
Butternut
Cedar

Aspen
Dogwood
Alder
Beech
Hawthorn
Tulip

## Environment

Location / GPS: _____  Date _____

Season:  ○ Spring  ○ Summer  ○ Fall  ○ Winter

Surroundings:  ○ Hedgerows  ○ Field  ○ Park  ○ Woodland  ○ Water
○ Other _____

Setting:  ○ Natural  ○ Artificial    Type:  ○ Evergreen  ○ Deciduous

Notes: _____
_____
_____

## General

Shape:  ○ Vase  ○ Columnar  ○ Round  ○ (Other) _____

Features:  ○ Conical/Spire  ○ Spreading  ○ Upright  ○ Weeping
○ (Other) _____

Branching:  ○ Opposite  ○ Alternate    Estimated Age: _____

Notes: _____
_____
_____

## Needles or Leaves

Type:  ○ Needle  ○ Simple Broadleaf  ○ Compound Broadleaf  ○ Scales

Shape:  ○ Cordate (heart-shaped)  ○ Lanceolate (long and narrow)
○ Deltoid (triangular)  ○ Obicular (round)  ○ Ovate (egg-shaped)
○ Palm and Maple  ○ Lobed

Structure:  ○ Simple (attached to twigs or twig stems)
○ Compound (attached to single lead steam)

Notes: _____
_____
_____

## Flowers, Fruits & Seeds

Flower Type:  ○ Single Blooms  ○ Clustered Blooms  ○ Catkins

Fruits / Seeds:  ○ Berries  ○ Apples  ○ Pears  ○ Nuts  ○ Acorns
○ Cones  ○ Capsules  ○ Catkins  ○ (Other) _____

Notes: _____
_____
_____

## Leaf Buds & Twigs

Bud Type:  ○ Terminal (grows at tip of a shoot causing shoot to grow longer)
○ Lateral (grow along sides of a shoot causing sideways growth)

Twig Features:  ○ Smooth  ○ Hairy  ○ Spines  ○ Corky Ribs
○ (Other) _____

Notes: _____
_____

## Bark

Texture:  ○ Furrowed  ○ Scaly  ○ Peeling  ○ Smooth  ○ Shiny
○ Fissured  ○ Ridges / Depressions  ○ Papery  ○ Warty
○ (Other) _____

Color:  ○ Gray  ○ Brown  ○ Cinnamon  ○ White  ○ Silver
○ Green  ○ Copper  ○ (Other) _____

Notes: _____

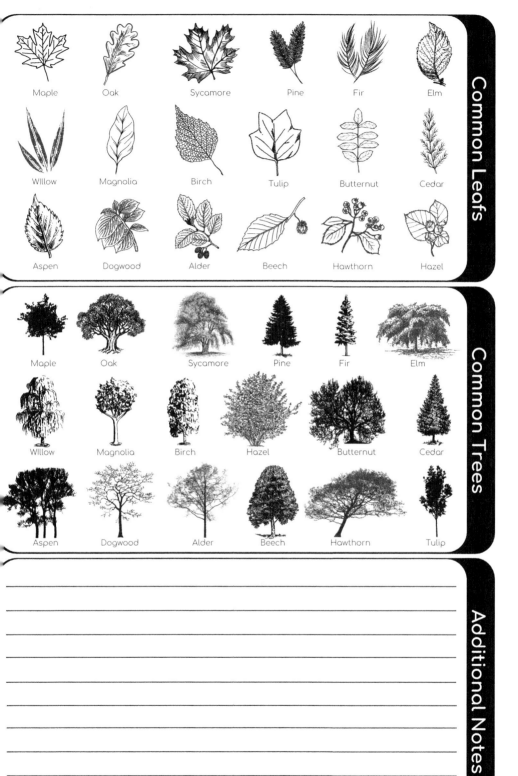

Maple  Oak  Sycamore  Pine  Fir  Elm

Wlllow  Magnolia  Birch  Tulip  Butternut  Cedar

Aspen  Dogwood  Alder  Beech  Hawthorn  Hazel

Maple  Oak  Sycamore  Pine  Fir  Elm

Wlllow  Magnolia  Birch  Hazel  Butternut  Cedar

Aspen  Dogwood  Alder  Beech  Hawthorn  Tulip

## Environment

Location / GPS: _____ Date _____

Season: ○ Spring    ○ Summer    ○ Fall    ○ Winter

Surroundings: ○ Hedgerows  ○ Field  ○ Park  ○ Woodland  ○ Water
              ○ Other_____

Setting: ○ Natural    ○ Artificial      Type: ○ Evergreen    ○ Deciduous

Notes:_____
_____

## General

Shape: ○ Vase  ○ Columnar  ○ Round  ○ (Other) _____

Features: ○ Conical/Spire  ○ Spreading  ○ Upright  ○ Weeping
          ○ (Other) _____

Branching: ○ Opposite  ○ Alternate      Estimated Age: _____

Notes: _____
_____

## Needles or Leaves

Type: ○ Needle  ○ Simple Broadleaf  ○ Compound Broadleaf  ○ Scales

Shape: ○ Cordate (heart-shaped)    ○ Lanceolate (long and narrow)
       ○ Deltoid (triangular)  ○ Obicular (round)  ○ Ovate (egg-shaped)
       ○ Palm and Maple    ○ Lobed

Structure: ○ Simple (attached to twigs or twig stems)
           ○ Compound (attached to single lead steam)

Notes: _____
_____

## Flowers, Fruits & Seeds

Flower Type: ○ Single Blooms   ○ Clustered Blooms   ○ Catkins

Fruits / Seeds: ○ Berries  ○ Apples  ○ Pears  ○ Nuts  ○ Acorns
                ○ Cones  ○ Capsules  ○ Catkins  ○ (Other) _____

Notes: _____
_____

## Leaf Buds & Twigs

Bud Type: ○ Terminal (grows at tip of a shoot causing shoot to grow longer)
          ○ Lateral (grow along sides of a shoot causing sideways growth)

Twig Features: ○ Smooth  ○ Hairy  ○ Spines  ○ Corky Ribs
               ○ (Other) _____

Notes: _____

## Bark

Texture: ○ Furrowed  ○ Scaly  ○ Peeling  ○ Smooth  ○ Shiny
         ○ Fissured  ○ Ridges / Depressions  ○ Papery  ○ Warty
         ○ (Other) _____

Color: ○ Gray  ○ Brown  ○ Cinnamon  ○ White  ○ Silver
       ○ Green  ○ Copper  ○ (Other) _____

Notes: _____

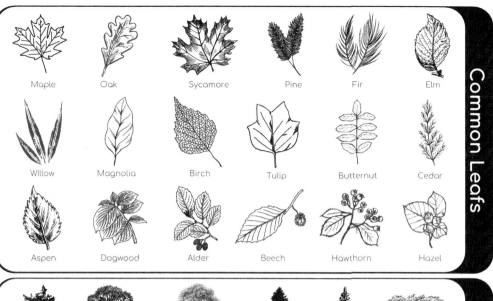

Maple    Oak    Sycamore    Pine    Fir    Elm

Wlllow    Magnolia    Birch    Tulip    Butternut    Cedar

Aspen    Dogwood    Alder    Beech    Hawthorn    Hazel

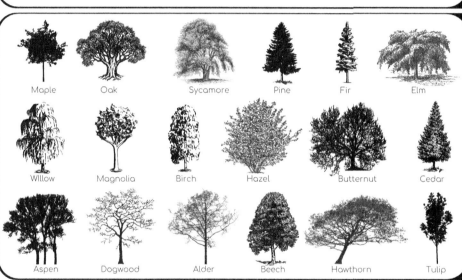

Maple    Oak    Sycamore    Pine    Fir    Elm

Wlllow    Magnolia    Birch    Hazel    Butternut    Cedar

Aspen    Dogwood    Alder    Beech    Hawthorn    Tulip

## Environment

Location / GPS: _____ Date _____

Season: ○ Spring ○ Summer ○ Fall ○ Winter

Surroundings: ○ Hedgerows ○ Field ○ Park ○ Woodland ○ Water
○ Other _____

Setting: ○ Natural ○ Artificial    Type: ○ Evergreen ○ Deciduous

Notes: _____
_____

## General

Shape: ○ Vase ○ Columnar ○ Round ○ (Other) _____

Features: ○ Conical/Spire ○ Spreading ○ Upright ○ Weeping
○ (Other) _____

Branching: ○ Opposite ○ Alternate    Estimated Age: _____

Notes: _____
_____

## Needles or Leaves

Type: ○ Needle ○ Simple Broadleaf ○ Compound Broadleaf ○ Scales

Shape: ○ Cordate (heart-shaped) ○ Lanceolate (long and narrow)
○ Deltoid (triangular) ○ Obicular (round) ○ Ovate (egg-shaped)
○ Palm and Maple ○ Lobed

Structure: ○ Simple (attached to twigs or twig stems)
○ Compound (attached to single lead steam)

Notes: _____
_____

## Flowers, Fruits & Seeds

Flower Type: ○ Single Blooms ○ Clustered Blooms ○ Catkins

Fruits / Seeds: ○ Berries ○ Apples ○ Pears ○ Nuts ○ Acorns
○ Cones ○ Capsules ○ Catkins ○ (Other) _____

Notes: _____
_____

## Leaf Buds & Twigs

Bud Type: ○ Terminal (grows at tip of a shoot causing shoot to grow longer)
○ Lateral (grow along sides of a shoot causing sideways growth)

Twig Features: ○ Smooth ○ Hairy ○ Spines ○ Corky Ribs
○ (Other) _____

Notes: _____

## Bark

Texture: ○ Furrowed ○ Scaly ○ Peeling ○ Smooth ○ Shiny
○ Fissured ○ Ridges / Depressions ○ Papery ○ Warty
○ (Other) _____

Color: ○ Gray ○ Brown ○ Cinnamon ○ White ○ Silver
○ Green ○ Copper ○ (Other) _____

Notes: _____

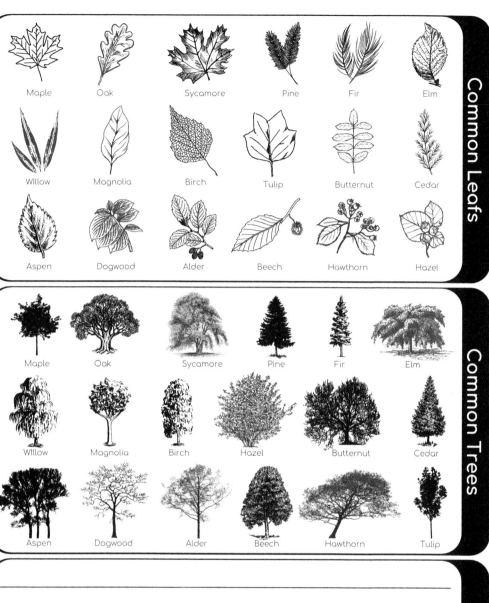

Maple · Oak · Sycamore · Pine · Fir · Elm

Willow · Magnolia · Birch · Tulip · Butternut · Cedar

Aspen · Dogwood · Alder · Beech · Hawthorn · Hazel

Maple · Oak · Sycamore · Pine · Fir · Elm

Willow · Magnolia · Birch · Hazel · Butternut · Cedar

Aspen · Dogwood · Alder · Beech · Hawthorn · Tulip

## Environment

Location / GPS: _____ Date _____

Season: ○ Spring ○ Summer ○ Fall ○ Winter

Surroundings: ○ Hedgerows ○ Field ○ Park ○ Woodland ○ Water
○ Other _____

Setting: ○ Natural ○ Artificial    Type: ○ Evergreen ○ Deciduous

Notes: _____
_____

## General

Shape: ○ Vase ○ Columnar ○ Round ○ (Other) _____

Features: ○ Conical/Spire ○ Spreading ○ Upright ○ Weeping
○ (Other) _____

Branching: ○ Opposite ○ Alternate    Estimated Age: _____

Notes: _____
_____

## Needles or Leaves

Type: ○ Needle ○ Simple Broadleaf ○ Compound Broadleaf ○ Scales

Shape: ○ Cordate (heart-shaped) ○ Lanceolate (long and narrow)
○ Deltoid (triangular) ○ Obicular (round) ○ Ovate (egg-shaped)
○ Palm and Maple ○ Lobed

Structure: ○ Simple (attached to twigs or twig stems)
○ Compound (attached to single lead steam)

Notes: _____
_____

## Flowers, Fruits & Seeds

Flower Type: ○ Single Blooms ○ Clustered Blooms ○ Catkins

Fruits / Seeds: ○ Berries ○ Apples ○ Pears ○ Nuts ○ Acorns
○ Cones ○ Capsules ○ Catkins ○ (Other) _____

Notes: _____
_____

## Leaf Buds & Twigs

Bud Type: ○ Terminal (grows at tip of a shoot causing shoot to grow longer)
○ Lateral (grow along sides of a shoot causing sideways growth)

Twig Features: ○ Smooth ○ Hairy ○ Spines ○ Corky Ribs
○ (Other) _____

Notes: _____

## Bark

Texture: ○ Furrowed ○ Scaly ○ Peeling ○ Smooth ○ Shiny
○ Fissured ○ Ridges / Depressions ○ Papery ○ Warty
○ (Other) _____

Color: ○ Gray ○ Brown ○ Cinnamon ○ White ○ Silver
○ Green ○ Copper ○ (Other) _____

Notes: _____

Maple | Oak | Sycamore | Pine | Fir | Elm

Willow | Magnolia | Birch | Tulip | Butternut | Cedar

Aspen | Dogwood | Alder | Beech | Hawthorn | Hazel

Maple | Oak | Sycamore | Pine | Fir | Elm

Willow | Magnolia | Birch | Hazel | Butternut | Cedar

Aspen | Dogwood | Alder | Beech | Hawthorn | Tulip

## Environment

Location / GPS: _____ Date _____

Season: ○ Spring ○ Summer ○ Fall ○ Winter

Surroundings: ○ Hedgerows ○ Field ○ Park ○ Woodland ○ Water
○ Other _____

Setting: ○ Natural ○ Artificial    Type: ○ Evergreen ○ Deciduous

Notes: _____
_____

## General

Shape: ○ Vase ○ Columnar ○ Round ○ (Other) _____

Features: ○ Conical/Spire ○ Spreading ○ Upright ○ Weeping
○ (Other) _____

Branching: ○ Opposite ○ Alternate    Estimated Age: _____

Notes: _____
_____

## Needles or Leaves

Type: ○ Needle ○ Simple Broadleaf ○ Compound Broadleaf ○ Scales

Shape: ○ Cordate (heart-shaped) ○ Lanceolate (long and narrow)
○ Deltoid (triangular) ○ Obicular (round) ○ Ovate (egg-shaped)
○ Palm and Maple ○ Lobed

Structure: ○ Simple (attached to twigs or twig stems)
○ Compound (attached to single lead steam)

Notes: _____
_____

## Flowers, Fruits & Seeds

Flower Type: ○ Single Blooms ○ Clustered Blooms ○ Catkins

Fruits / Seeds: ○ Berries ○ Apples ○ Pears ○ Nuts ○ Acorns
○ Cones ○ Capsules ○ Catkins ○ (Other) _____

Notes: _____
_____

## Leaf Buds & Twigs

Bud Type: ○ Terminal (grows at tip of a shoot causing shoot to grow longer)
○ Lateral (grow along sides of a shoot causing sideways growth)

Twig Features: ○ Smooth ○ Hairy ○ Spines ○ Corky Ribs
○ (Other) _____

Notes: _____

## Bark

Texture: ○ Furrowed ○ Scaly ○ Peeling ○ Smooth ○ Shiny
○ Fissured ○ Ridges / Depressions ○ Papery ○ Warty
○ (Other) _____

Color: ○ Gray ○ Brown ○ Cinnamon ○ White ○ Silver
○ Green ○ Copper ○ (Other) _____

Notes: _____

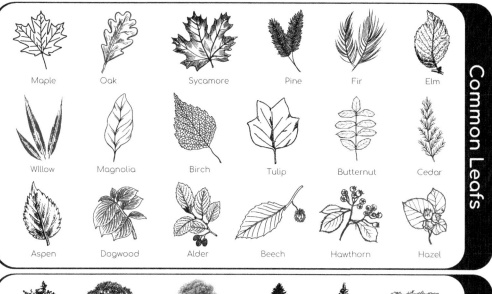

Maple Oak Sycamore Pine Fir Elm

WIllow Magnolia Birch Tulip Butternut Cedar

Aspen Dogwood Alder Beech Hawthorn Hazel

Maple Oak Sycamore Pine Fir Elm

WIllow Magnolia Birch Hazel Butternut Cedar

Aspen Dogwood Alder Beech Hawthorn Tulip

## Environment

Location / GPS: _____ Date _____

Season: ○ Spring ○ Summer ○ Fall ○ Winter

Surroundings: ○ Hedgerows ○ Field ○ Park ○ Woodland ○ Water
○ Other _____

Setting: ○ Natural ○ Artificial    Type: ○ Evergreen ○ Deciduous

Notes: _____
_____

## General

Shape: ○ Vase ○ Columnar ○ Round ○ (Other) _____

Features: ○ Conical/Spire ○ Spreading ○ Upright ○ Weeping
○ (Other) _____

Branching: ○ Opposite ○ Alternate    Estimated Age: _____

Notes: _____
_____

## Needles or Leaves

Type: ○ Needle ○ Simple Broadleaf ○ Compound Broadleaf ○ Scales

Shape: ○ Cordate (heart-shaped) ○ Lanceolate (long and narrow)
○ Deltoid (triangular) ○ Obicular (round) ○ Ovate (egg-shaped)
○ Palm and Maple ○ Lobed

Structure: ○ Simple (attached to twigs or twig stems)
○ Compound (attached to single lead steam)

Notes: _____
_____

## Flowers, Fruits & Seeds

Flower Type: ○ Single Blooms ○ Clustered Blooms ○ Catkins

Fruits / Seeds: ○ Berries ○ Apples ○ Pears ○ Nuts ○ Acorns
○ Cones ○ Capsules ○ Catkins ○ (Other) _____

Notes: _____
_____

## Leaf Buds & Twigs

Bud Type: ○ Terminal (grows at tip of a shoot causing shoot to grow longer)
○ Lateral (grow along sides of a shoot causing sideways growth)

Twig Features: ○ Smooth ○ Hairy ○ Spines ○ Corky Ribs
○ (Other) _____

Notes: _____

## Bark

Texture: ○ Furrowed ○ Scaly ○ Peeling ○ Smooth ○ Shiny
○ Fissured ○ Ridges / Depressions ○ Papery ○ Warty
○ (Other) _____

Color: ○ Gray ○ Brown ○ Cinnamon ○ White ○ Silver
○ Green ○ Copper ○ (Other) _____

Notes: _____

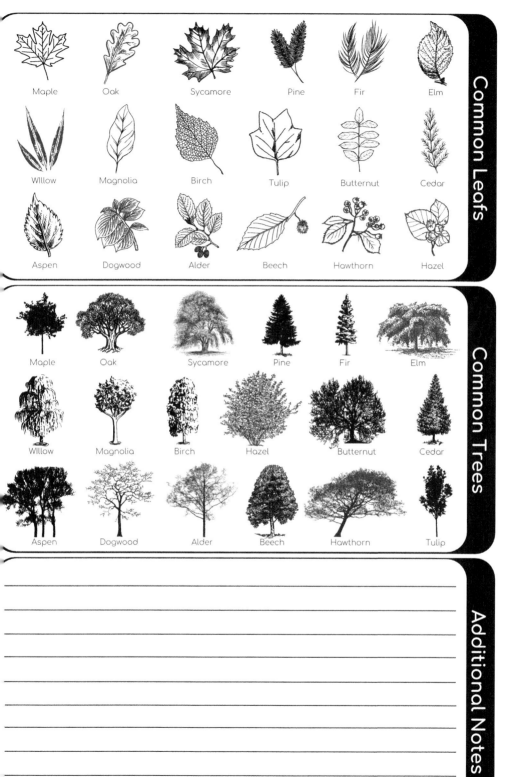

Maple    Oak    Sycamore    Pine    Fir    Elm

WIllow    Magnolia    Birch    Tulip    Butternut    Cedar

Aspen    Dogwood    Alder    Beech    Hawthorn    Hazel

Maple    Oak    Sycamore    Pine    Fir    Elm

WIllow    Magnolia    Birch    Hazel    Butternut    Cedar

Aspen    Dogwood    Alder    Beech    Hawthorn    Tulip

## Environment

Location / GPS: _____ Date _____

Season: ○ Spring ○ Summer ○ Fall ○ Winter

Surroundings: ○ Hedgerows ○ Field ○ Park ○ Woodland ○ Water
○ Other _____

Setting: ○ Natural ○ Artificial **Type:** ○ Evergreen ○ Deciduous

Notes: _____
_____

## General

Shape: ○ Vase ○ Columnar ○ Round ○ (Other) _____

Features: ○ Conical/Spire ○ Spreading ○ Upright ○ Weeping
○ (Other) _____

Branching: ○ Opposite ○ Alternate **Estimated Age:** _____

Notes: _____
_____

## Needles or Leaves

Type: ○ Needle ○ Simple Broadleaf ○ Compound Broadleaf ○ Scales

Shape: ○ Cordate (heart-shaped) ○ Lanceolate (long and narrow)
○ Deltoid (triangular) ○ Obicular (round) ○ Ovate (egg-shaped)
○ Palm and Maple ○ Lobed

Structure: ○ Simple (attached to twigs or twig stems)
○ Compound (attached to single lead steam)

Notes: _____
_____

## Flowers, Fruits & Seeds

Flower Type: ○ Single Blooms ○ Clustered Blooms ○ Catkins

Fruits / Seeds: ○ Berries ○ Apples ○ Pears ○ Nuts ○ Acorns
○ Cones ○ Capsules ○ Catkins ○ (Other) _____

Notes: _____
_____

## Leaf Buds & Twigs

Bud Type: ○ Terminal (grows at tip of a shoot causing shoot to grow longer)
○ Lateral (grow along sides of a shoot causing sideways growth)

Twig Features: ○ Smooth ○ Hairy ○ Spines ○ Corky Ribs
○ (Other) _____

Notes: _____

## Bark

Texture: ○ Furrowed ○ Scaly ○ Peeling ○ Smooth ○ Shiny
○ Fissured ○ Ridges / Depressions ○ Papery ○ Warty
○ (Other) _____

Color: ○ Gray ○ Brown ○ Cinnamon ○ White ○ Silver
○ Green ○ Copper ○ (Other) _____

Notes: _____

Maple  Oak  Sycamore  Pine  Fir  Elm

WIllow  Magnolia  Birch  Tulip  Butternut  Cedar

Aspen  Dogwood  Alder  Beech  Hawthorn  Hazel

Maple  Oak  Sycamore  Pine  Fir  Elm

WIllow  Magnolia  Birch  Hazel  Butternut  Cedar

Aspen  Dogwood  Alder  Beech  Hawthorn  Tulip

## Environment

Location / GPS: _____ Date _____

Season: ○ Spring ○ Summer ○ Fall ○ Winter

Surroundings: ○ Hedgerows ○ Field ○ Park ○ Woodland ○ Water
○ Other _____

Setting: ○ Natural ○ Artificial     Type: ○ Evergreen ○ Deciduous

Notes: _____
_____

## General

Shape: ○ Vase ○ Columnar ○ Round ○ (Other) _____

Features: ○ Conical/Spire ○ Spreading ○ Upright ○ Weeping
○ (Other) _____

Branching: ○ Opposite ○ Alternate     Estimated Age: _____

Notes: _____
_____

## Needles or Leaves

Type: ○ Needle ○ Simple Broadleaf ○ Compound Broadleaf ○ Scales

Shape: ○ Cordate (heart-shaped) ○ Lanceolate (long and narrow)
○ Deltoid (triangular) ○ Obicular (round) ○ Ovate (egg-shaped)
○ Palm and Maple ○ Lobed

Structure: ○ Simple (attached to twigs or twig stems)
○ Compound (attached to single lead steam)

Notes: _____
_____

## Flowers, Fruits & Seeds

Flower Type: ○ Single Blooms ○ Clustered Blooms ○ Catkins

Fruits / Seeds: ○ Berries ○ Apples ○ Pears ○ Nuts ○ Acorns
○ Cones ○ Capsules ○ Catkins ○ (Other) _____

Notes: _____
_____

## Leaf Buds & Twigs

Bud Type: ○ Terminal (grows at tip of a shoot causing shoot to grow longer)
○ Lateral (grow along sides of a shoot causing sideways growth)

Twig Features: ○ Smooth ○ Hairy ○ Spines ○ Corky Ribs
○ (Other) _____

Notes: _____

## Bark

Texture: ○ Furrowed ○ Scaly ○ Peeling ○ Smooth ○ Shiny
○ Fissured ○ Ridges / Depressions ○ Papery ○ Warty
○ (Other) _____

Color: ○ Gray ○ Brown ○ Cinnamon ○ White ○ Silver
○ Green ○ Copper ○ (Other) _____

Notes: _____

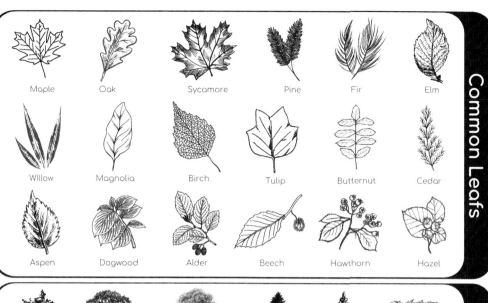

Maple — Oak — Sycamore — Pine — Fir — Elm

Willow — Magnolia — Birch — Tulip — Butternut — Cedar

Aspen — Dogwood — Alder — Beech — Hawthorn — Hazel

Maple — Oak — Sycamore — Pine — Fir — Elm

Willow — Magnolia — Birch — Hazel — Butternut — Cedar

Aspen — Dogwood — Alder — Beech — Hawthorn — Tulip

## Environment

Location / GPS: _____ Date _____

Season: ○ Spring  ○ Summer  ○ Fall  ○ Winter

Surroundings: ○ Hedgerows  ○ Field  ○ Park  ○ Woodland  ○ Water
○ Other _____

Setting: ○ Natural  ○ Artificial  **Type:** ○ Evergreen  ○ Deciduous

Notes: _____
_____

## General

Shape: ○ Vase  ○ Columnar  ○ Round  ○ (Other) _____

Features: ○ Conical/Spire  ○ Spreading  ○ Upright  ○ Weeping
○ (Other) _____

Branching: ○ Opposite  ○ Alternate  **Estimated Age:** _____

Notes: _____
_____

## Needles or Leaves

Type: ○ Needle  ○ Simple Broadleaf  ○ Compound Broadleaf  ○ Scales

Shape: ○ Cordate (heart-shaped)  ○ Lanceolate (long and narrow)
○ Deltoid (triangular)  ○ Obicular (round)  ○ Ovate (egg-shaped)
○ Palm and Maple  ○ Lobed

Structure: ○ Simple (attached to twigs or twig stems)
○ Compound (attached to single lead steam)

Notes: _____
_____

## Flowers, Fruits & Seeds

Flower Type: ○ Single Blooms  ○ Clustered Blooms  ○ Catkins

Fruits / Seeds: ○ Berries  ○ Apples  ○ Pears  ○ Nuts  ○ Acorns
○ Cones  ○ Capsules  ○ Catkins  ○ (Other) _____

Notes: _____
_____

## Leaf Buds & Twigs

Bud Type: ○ Terminal (grows at tip of a shoot causing shoot to grow longer)
○ Lateral (grow along sides of a shoot causing sideways growth)

Twig Features: ○ Smooth  ○ Hairy  ○ Spines  ○ Corky Ribs
○ (Other) _____

Notes: _____

## Bark

Texture: ○ Furrowed  ○ Scaly  ○ Peeling  ○ Smooth  ○ Shiny
○ Fissured  ○ Ridges / Depressions  ○ Papery  ○ Warty
○ (Other) _____

Color: ○ Gray  ○ Brown  ○ Cinnamon  ○ White  ○ Silver
○ Green  ○ Copper  ○ (Other) _____

Notes: _____

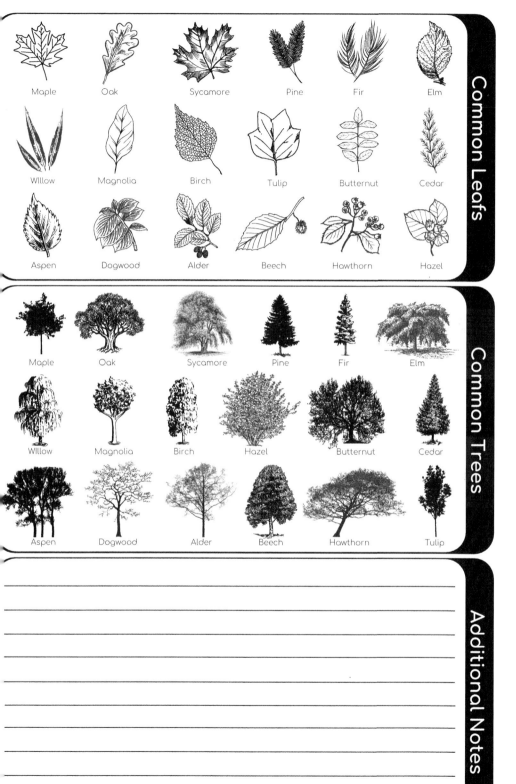

Maple
Oak
Sycamore
Pine
Fir
Elm

Wlllow
Magnolia
Birch
Tulip
Butternut
Cedar

Aspen
Dogwood
Alder
Beech
Hawthorn
Hazel

Maple
Oak
Sycamore
Pine
Fir
Elm

Wlllow
Magnolia
Birch
Hazel
Butternut
Cedar

Aspen
Dogwood
Alder
Beech
Hawthorn
Tulip

## Environment

Location / GPS: _____  Date _____

Season:  ○ Spring   ○ Summer   ○ Fall   ○ Winter

Surroundings:  ○ Hedgerows   ○ Field   ○ Park   ○ Woodland   ○ Water
○ Other_____

Setting:  ○ Natural   ○ Artificial      **Type:** ○ Evergreen   ○ Deciduous

Notes: _____
_____

## General

Shape:  ○ Vase   ○ Columnar   ○ Round   ○ (Other) _____

Features:  ○ Conical/Spire   ○ Spreading   ○ Upright   ○ Weeping
○ (Other) _____

Branching:  ○ Opposite   ○ Alternate      **Estimated Age:** _____

Notes: _____
_____

## Needles or Leaves

Type:  ○ Needle   ○ Simple Broadleaf   ○ Compound Broadleaf   ○ Scales

Shape:  ○ Cordate (heart-shaped)   ○ Lanceolate (long and narrow)
○ Deltoid (triangular)  ○ Obicular (round)   ○ Ovate (egg-shaped)
○ Palm and Maple   ○ Lobed

Structure:  ○ Simple (attached to twigs or twig stems)
○ Compound (attached to single lead steam)

Notes: _____
_____

## Flowers, Fruits & Seeds

Flower Type:  ○ Single Blooms   ○ Clustered Blooms   ○ Catkins

Fruits / Seeds:  ○ Berries   ○ Apples   ○ Pears   ○ Nuts   ○ Acorns
○ Cones   ○ Capsules   ○ Catkins   ○ (Other) _____

Notes: _____
_____

## Leaf Buds & Twigs

Bud Type:  ○ Terminal (grows at tip of a shoot causing shoot to grow longer)
○ Lateral (grow along sides of a shoot causing sideways growth)

Twig Features:  ○ Smooth  ○ Hairy   ○ Spines   ○ Corky Ribs
○ (Other) _____

Notes: _____

## Bark

Texture:  ○ Furrowed  ○ Scaly  ○ Peeling  ○ Smooth  ○ Shiny
○ Fissured  ○ Ridges / Depressions  ○ Papery  ○ Warty
○ (Other) _____

Color:  ○ Gray  ○ Brown   ○ Cinnamon   ○ White   ○ Silver
○ Green  ○ Copper  ○ (Other) _____

Notes: _____

Maple · Oak · Sycamore · Pine · Fir · Elm
Willow · Magnolia · Birch · Tulip · Butternut · Cedar
Aspen · Dogwood · Alder · Beech · Hawthorn · Hazel

Maple · Oak · Sycamore · Pine · Fir · Elm
Willow · Magnolia · Birch · Hazel · Butternut · Cedar
Aspen · Dogwood · Alder · Beech · Hawthorn · Tulip

## Environment

Location / GPS: _____  Date _____

Season: ○ Spring  ○ Summer  ○ Fall  ○ Winter

Surroundings: ○ Hedgerows  ○ Field  ○ Park  ○ Woodland  ○ Water
○ Other_____

Setting: ○ Natural  ○ Artificial  **Type:** ○ Evergreen  ○ Deciduous

Notes: _____
_____
_____

## General

Shape: ○ Vase  ○ Columnar  ○ Round  ○ (Other) _____

Features: ○ Conical/Spire  ○ Spreading  ○ Upright  ○ Weeping
○ (Other) _____

Branching: ○ Opposite  ○ Alternate  **Estimated Age:** _____

Notes: _____
_____
_____

## Needles or Leaves

Type: ○ Needle  ○ Simple Broadleaf  ○ Compound Broadleaf  ○ Scales

Shape: ○ Cordate (heart-shaped)  ○ Lanceolate (long and narrow)
○ Deltoid (triangular)  ○ Obicular (round)  ○ Ovate (egg-shaped)
○ Palm and Maple  ○ Lobed

Structure: ○ Simple (attached to twigs or twig stems)
○ Compound (attached to single lead steam)

Notes: _____
_____
_____

## Flowers, Fruits & Seeds

Flower Type: ○ Single Blooms  ○ Clustered Blooms  ○ Catkins

Fruits / Seeds: ○ Berries  ○ Apples  ○ Pears  ○ Nuts  ○ Acorns
○ Cones  ○ Capsules  ○ Catkins  ○ (Other) _____

Notes: _____
_____
_____

## Leaf Buds & Twigs

Bud Type: ○ Terminal (grows at tip of a shoot causing shoot to grow longer)
○ Lateral (grow along sides of a shoot causing sideways growth)

Twig Features: ○ Smooth  ○ Hairy  ○ Spines  ○ Corky Ribs
○ (Other) _____

Notes: _____
_____

## Bark

Texture: ○ Furrowed  ○ Scaly  ○ Peeling  ○ Smooth  ○ Shiny
○ Fissured  ○ Ridges / Depressions  ○ Papery  ○ Warty
○ (Other) _____

Color: ○ Gray  ○ Brown  ○ Cinnamon  ○ White  ○ Silver
○ Green  ○ Copper  ○ (Other) _____

Notes: _____

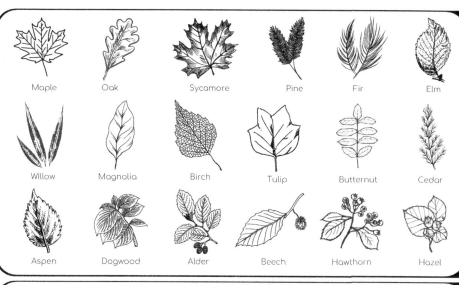

Maple · Oak · Sycamore · Pine · Fir · Elm
Willow · Magnolia · Birch · Tulip · Butternut · Cedar
Aspen · Dogwood · Alder · Beech · Hawthorn · Hazel

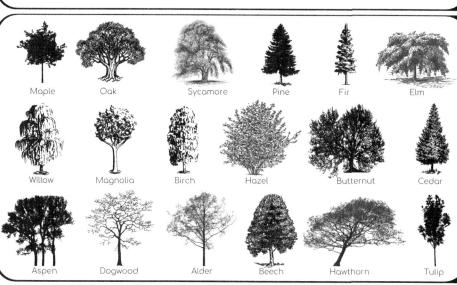

Maple · Oak · Sycamore · Pine · Fir · Elm
Willow · Magnolia · Birch · Hazel · Butternut · Cedar
Aspen · Dogwood · Alder · Beech · Hawthorn · Tulip

## Environment

Location / GPS: _____ Date _____

Season: ○ Spring   ○ Summer   ○ Fall   ○ Winter

Surroundings: ○ Hedgerows   ○ Field   ○ Park   ○ Woodland   ○ Water
○ Other _____

Setting: ○ Natural   ○ Artificial       Type: ○ Evergreen   ○ Deciduous

Notes: _____
_____

## General

Shape: ○ Vase   ○ Columnar   ○ Round   ○ (Other) _____

Features: ○ Conical/Spire   ○ Spreading   ○ Upright   ○ Weeping
○ (Other) _____

Branching: ○ Opposite   ○ Alternate       Estimated Age: _____

Notes: _____
_____

## Needles or Leaves

Type: ○ Needle   ○ Simple Broadleaf   ○ Compound Broadleaf   ○ Scales

Shape: ○ Cordate (heart-shaped)   ○ Lanceolate (long and narrow)
○ Deltoid (triangular)   ○ Obicular (round)   ○ Ovate (egg-shaped)
○ Palm and Maple   ○ Lobed

Structure: ○ Simple (attached to twigs or twig stems)
○ Compound (attached to single lead steam)

Notes: _____
_____

## Flowers, Fruits & Seeds

Flower Type: ○ Single Blooms   ○ Clustered Blooms   ○ Catkins

Fruits / Seeds: ○ Berries   ○ Apples   ○ Pears   ○ Nuts   ○ Acorns
○ Cones   ○ Capsules   ○ Catkins   ○ (Other) _____

Notes: _____
_____

## Leaf Buds & Twigs

Bud Type: ○ Terminal (grows at tip of a shoot causing shoot to grow longer)
○ Lateral (grow along sides of a shoot causing sideways growth)

Twig Features: ○ Smooth   ○ Hairy   ○ Spines   ○ Corky Ribs
○ (Other) _____

Notes: _____

## Bark

Texture: ○ Furrowed   ○ Scaly   ○ Peeling   ○ Smooth   ○ Shiny
○ Fissured   ○ Ridges / Depressions   ○ Papery   ○ Warty
○ (Other) _____

Color: ○ Gray   ○ Brown   ○ Cinnamon   ○ White   ○ Silver
○ Green   ○ Copper   ○ (Other) _____

Notes: _____

| | | | | | |
|---|---|---|---|---|---|
| Maple | Oak | Sycamore | Pine | Fir | Elm |
| WIllow | Magnolia | Birch | Tulip | Butternut | Cedar |
| Aspen | Dogwood | Alder | Beech | Hawthorn | Hazel |

| | | | | | |
|---|---|---|---|---|---|
| Maple | Oak | Sycamore | Pine | Fir | Elm |
| WIllow | Magnolia | Birch | Hazel | Butternut | Cedar |
| Aspen | Dogwood | Alder | Beech | Hawthorn | Tulip |

## Environment

Location / GPS: _____ Date _____

Season: ○ Spring ○ Summer ○ Fall ○ Winter

Surroundings: ○ Hedgerows ○ Field ○ Park ○ Woodland ○ Water
○ Other _____

Setting: ○ Natural ○ Artificial   Type: ○ Evergreen ○ Deciduous

Notes: _____
_____

## General

Shape: ○ Vase ○ Columnar ○ Round ○ (Other) _____

Features: ○ Conical/Spire ○ Spreading ○ Upright ○ Weeping
○ (Other) _____

Branching: ○ Opposite ○ Alternate   Estimated Age: _____

Notes: _____
_____

## Needles or Leaves

Type: ○ Needle ○ Simple Broadleaf ○ Compound Broadleaf ○ Scales

Shape: ○ Cordate (heart-shaped) ○ Lanceolate (long and narrow)
○ Deltoid (triangular) ○ Obicular (round) ○ Ovate (egg-shaped)
○ Palm and Maple ○ Lobed

Structure: ○ Simple (attached to twigs or twig stems)
○ Compound (attached to single lead steam)

Notes: _____
_____

## Flowers, Fruits & Seeds

Flower Type: ○ Single Blooms ○ Clustered Blooms ○ Catkins

Fruits / Seeds: ○ Berries ○ Apples ○ Pears ○ Nuts ○ Acorns
○ Cones ○ Capsules ○ Catkins ○ (Other) _____

Notes: _____
_____

## Leaf Buds & Twigs

Bud Type: ○ Terminal (grows at tip of a shoot causing shoot to grow longer)
○ Lateral (grow along sides of a shoot causing sideways growth)

Twig Features: ○ Smooth ○ Hairy ○ Spines ○ Corky Ribs
○ (Other) _____

Notes: _____

## Bark

Texture: ○ Furrowed ○ Scaly ○ Peeling ○ Smooth ○ Shiny
○ Fissured ○ Ridges / Depressions ○ Papery ○ Warty
○ (Other) _____

Color: ○ Gray ○ Brown ○ Cinnamon ○ White ○ Silver
○ Green ○ Copper ○ (Other) _____

Notes: _____

| | | | | | |
|---|---|---|---|---|---|
| Maple | Oak | Sycamore | Pine | Fir | Elm |
| WIllow | Magnolia | Birch | Tulip | Butternut | Cedar |
| Aspen | Dogwood | Alder | Beech | Hawthorn | Hazel |

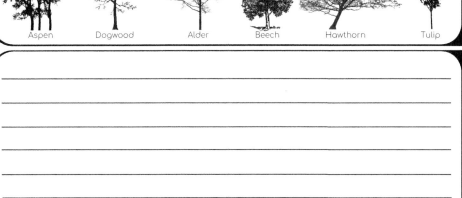

| | | | | | |
|---|---|---|---|---|---|
| Maple | Oak | Sycamore | Pine | Fir | Elm |
| WIllow | Magnolia | Birch | Hazel | Butternut | Cedar |
| Aspen | Dogwood | Alder | Beech | Hawthorn | Tulip |

## Environment

Location / GPS: _____ Date _____

Season: ○ Spring ○ Summer ○ Fall ○ Winter

Surroundings: ○ Hedgerows ○ Field ○ Park ○ Woodland ○ Water
○ Other _____

Setting: ○ Natural ○ Artificial  Type: ○ Evergreen ○ Deciduous

Notes: _____
_____
_____

## General

Shape: ○ Vase ○ Columnar ○ Round ○ (Other) _____

Features: ○ Conical/Spire ○ Spreading ○ Upright ○ Weeping
○ (Other) _____

Branching: ○ Opposite ○ Alternate  Estimated Age: _____

Notes: _____
_____
_____

## Needles or Leaves

Type: ○ Needle ○ Simple Broadleaf ○ Compound Broadleaf ○ Scales

Shape: ○ Cordate (heart-shaped) ○ Lanceolate (long and narrow)
○ Deltoid (triangular) ○ Obicular (round) ○ Ovate (egg-shaped)
○ Palm and Maple ○ Lobed

Structure: ○ Simple (attached to twigs or twig stems)
○ Compound (attached to single lead steam)

Notes: _____
_____
_____

## Flowers, Fruits & Seeds

Flower Type: ○ Single Blooms ○ Clustered Blooms ○ Catkins

Fruits / Seeds: ○ Berries ○ Apples ○ Pears ○ Nuts ○ Acorns
○ Cones ○ Capsules ○ Catkins ○ (Other) _____

Notes: _____
_____
_____

## Leaf Buds & Twigs

Bud Type: ○ Terminal (grows at tip of a shoot causing shoot to grow longer)
○ Lateral (grow along sides of a shoot causing sideways growth)

Twig Features: ○ Smooth ○ Hairy ○ Spines ○ Corky Ribs
○ (Other) _____

Notes: _____
_____

## Bark

Texture: ○ Furrowed ○ Scaly ○ Peeling ○ Smooth ○ Shiny
○ Fissured ○ Ridges / Depressions ○ Papery ○ Warty
○ (Other) _____

Color: ○ Gray ○ Brown ○ Cinnamon ○ White ○ Silver
○ Green ○ Copper ○ (Other) _____

Notes: _____
_____

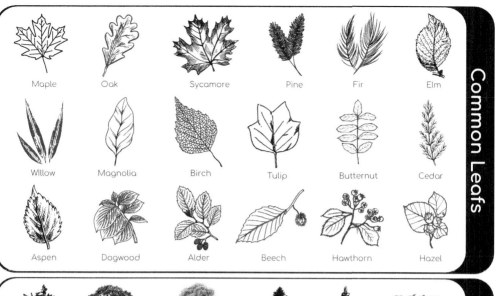

Maple  Oak  Sycamore  Pine  Fir  Elm

WIllow  Magnolia  Birch  Tulip  Butternut  Cedar

Aspen  Dogwood  Alder  Beech  Hawthorn  Hazel

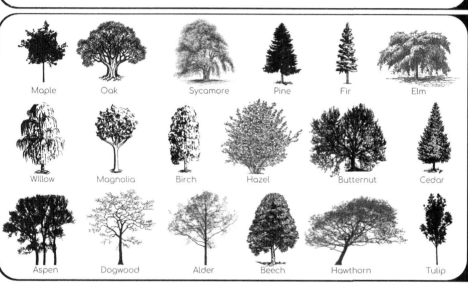

Maple  Oak  Sycamore  Pine  Fir  Elm

WIllow  Magnolia  Birch  Hazel  Butternut  Cedar

Aspen  Dogwood  Alder  Beech  Hawthorn  Tulip

## Environment

Location / GPS: _____ Date _____

Season: ○ Spring ○ Summer ○ Fall ○ Winter

Surroundings: ○ Hedgerows ○ Field ○ Park ○ Woodland ○ Water
○ Other_____

Setting: ○ Natural ○ Artificial **Type:** ○ Evergreen ○ Deciduous

Notes: _____
_____

## General

Shape: ○ Vase ○ Columnar ○ Round ○ (Other) _____

Features: ○ Conical/Spire ○ Spreading ○ Upright ○ Weeping
○ (Other) _____

Branching: ○ Opposite ○ Alternate **Estimated Age:** _____

Notes: _____
_____

## Needles or Leaves

Type: ○ Needle ○ Simple Broadleaf ○ Compound Broadleaf ○ Scales

Shape: ○ Cordate (heart-shaped) ○ Lanceolate (long and narrow)
○ Deltoid (triangular) ○ Obicular (round) ○ Ovate (egg-shaped)
○ Palm and Maple ○ Lobed

Structure: ○ Simple (attached to twigs or twig stems)
○ Compound (attached to single lead steam)

Notes: _____
_____

## Flowers, Fruits & Seeds

Flower Type: ○ Single Blooms ○ Clustered Blooms ○ Catkins

Fruits / Seeds: ○ Berries ○ Apples ○ Pears ○ Nuts ○ Acorns
○ Cones ○ Capsules ○ Catkins ○ (Other) _____

Notes: _____
_____

## Leaf Buds & Twigs

Bud Type: ○ Terminal (grows at tip of a shoot causing shoot to grow longer)
○ Lateral (grow along sides of a shoot causing sideways growth)

Twig Features: ○ Smooth ○ Hairy ○ Spines ○ Corky Ribs
○ (Other) _____

Notes: _____

## Bark

Texture: ○ Furrowed ○ Scaly ○ Peeling ○ Smooth ○ Shiny
○ Fissured ○ Ridges / Depressions ○ Papery ○ Warty
○ (Other) _____

Color: ○ Gray ○ Brown ○ Cinnamon ○ White ○ Silver
○ Green ○ Copper ○ (Other) _____

Notes: _____

Maple
Oak
Sycamore
Pine
Fir
Elm

Wlllow
Magnolia
Birch
Tulip
Butternut
Cedar

Aspen
Dogwood
Alder
Beech
Hawthorn
Hazel

Maple
Oak
Sycamore
Pine
Fir
Elm

Wlllow
Magnolia
Birch
Hazel
Butternut
Cedar

Aspen
Dogwood
Alder
Beech
Hawthorn
Tulip

## Environment

Location / GPS: _____ Date _____

Season: ○ Spring  ○ Summer  ○ Fall  ○ Winter

Surroundings: ○ Hedgerows  ○ Field  ○ Park  ○ Woodland  ○ Water
○ Other_____

Setting: ○ Natural  ○ Artificial    Type: ○ Evergreen  ○ Deciduous

Notes: _____
_____
_____

## General

Shape: ○ Vase  ○ Columnar  ○ Round  ○ (Other) _____

Features: ○ Conical/Spire  ○ Spreading  ○ Upright  ○ Weeping
○ (Other) _____

Branching: ○ Opposite  ○ Alternate     Estimated Age: _____

Notes: _____
_____
_____

## Needles or Leaves

Type: ○ Needle  ○ Simple Broadleaf  ○ Compound Broadleaf  ○ Scales

Shape: ○ Cordate (heart-shaped)  ○ Lanceolate (long and narrow)
○ Deltoid (triangular)  ○ Obicular (round)  ○ Ovate (egg-shaped)
○ Palm and Maple  ○ Lobed

Structure: ○ Simple (attached to twigs or twig stems)
○ Compound (attached to single lead steam)

Notes: _____
_____
_____

## Flowers, Fruits & Seeds

Flower Type: ○ Single Blooms  ○ Clustered Blooms  ○ Catkins

Fruits / Seeds: ○ Berries  ○ Apples  ○ Pears  ○ Nuts  ○ Acorns
○ Cones  ○ Capsules  ○ Catkins  ○ (Other) _____

Notes: _____
_____
_____

## Leaf Buds & Twigs

Bud Type: ○ Terminal (grows at tip of a shoot causing shoot to grow longer)
○ Lateral (grow along sides of a shoot causing sideways growth)

Twig Features: ○ Smooth  ○ Hairy  ○ Spines  ○ Corky Ribs
○ (Other) _____

Notes: _____
_____

## Bark

Texture: ○ Furrowed  ○ Scaly  ○ Peeling  ○ Smooth  ○ Shiny
○ Fissured  ○ Ridges / Depressions  ○ Papery  ○ Warty
○ (Other) _____

Color: ○ Gray  ○ Brown  ○ Cinnamon  ○ White  ○ Silver
○ Green  ○ Copper  ○ (Other) _____

Notes: _____

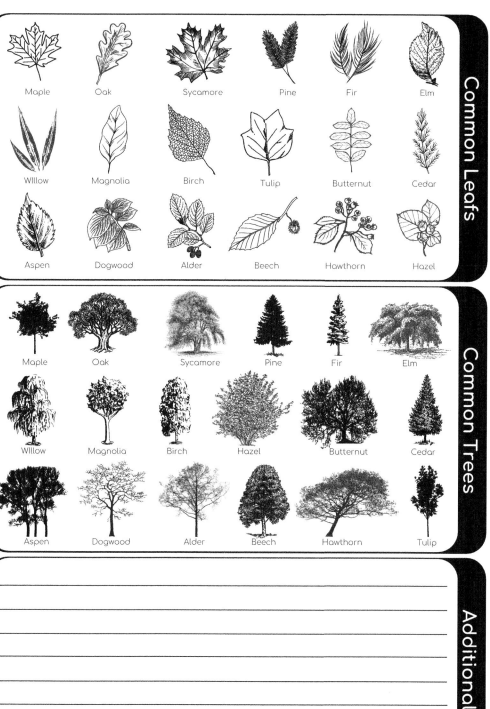

Maple    Oak    Sycamore    Pine    Fir    Elm

Wlllow    Magnolia    Birch    Tulip    Butternut    Cedar

Aspen    Dogwood    Alder    Beech    Hawthorn    Hazel

Maple    Oak    Sycamore    Pine    Fir    Elm

Wlllow    Magnolia    Birch    Hazel    Butternut    Cedar

Aspen    Dogwood    Alder    Beech    Hawthorn    Tulip

## Environment

Location / GPS: _____  Date _____

Season:  ◯ Spring   ◯ Summer   ◯ Fall   ◯ Winter

Surroundings:  ◯ Hedgerows  ◯ Field  ◯ Park  ◯ Woodland  ◯ Water
◯ Other_____

Setting:  ◯ Natural   ◯ Artificial      Type:  ◯ Evergreen   ◯ Deciduous

Notes:_____
_____

## General

Shape:  ◯ Vase  ◯ Columnar  ◯ Round  ◯ (Other) _____

Features:  ◯ Conical/Spire  ◯ Spreading  ◯ Upright  ◯ Weeping
◯ (Other) _____

Branching:  ◯ Opposite  ◯ Alternate      Estimated Age: _____

Notes: _____
_____

## Needles or Leaves

Type:  ◯ Needle  ◯ Simple Broadleaf  ◯ Compound Broadleaf  ◯ Scales

Shape:  ◯ Cordate (heart-shaped)   ◯ Lanceolate (long and narrow)
◯ Deltoid (triangular)  ◯ Obicular (round)  ◯ Ovate (egg-shaped)
◯ Palm and Maple   ◯ Lobed

Structure:  ◯ Simple (attached to twigs or twig stems)
◯ Compound (attached to single lead steam)

Notes: _____
_____

## Flowers, Fruits & Seeds

Flower Type:  ◯ Single Blooms   ◯ Clustered Blooms   ◯ Catkins

Fruits / Seeds:  ◯ Berries  ◯ Apples  ◯ Pears  ◯ Nuts  ◯ Acorns
◯ Cones  ◯ Capsules  ◯ Catkins  ◯ (Other) _____

Notes: _____
_____

## Leaf Buds & Twigs

Bud Type:  ◯ Terminal (grows at tip of a shoot causing shoot to grow longer)
◯ Lateral (grow along sides of a shoot causing sideways growth)

Twig Features:  ◯ Smooth  ◯ Hairy  ◯ Spines  ◯ Corky Ribs
◯ (Other) _____

Notes: _____

## Bark

Texture:  ◯ Furrowed  ◯ Scaly  ◯ Peeling  ◯ Smooth  ◯ Shiny
◯ Fissured  ◯ Ridges / Depressions  ◯ Papery  ◯ Warty
◯ (Other) _____

Color:  ◯ Gray  ◯ Brown  ◯ Cinnamon  ◯ White  ◯ Silver
◯ Green  ◯ Copper  ◯ (Other) _____

Notes: _____

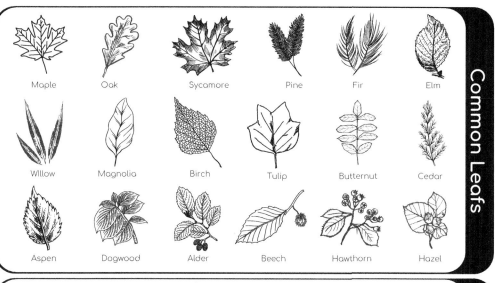

| | | | | | |
|---|---|---|---|---|---|
| Maple | Oak | Sycamore | Pine | Fir | Elm |
| Wlllow | Magnolia | Birch | Tulip | Butternut | Cedar |
| Aspen | Dogwood | Alder | Beech | Hawthorn | Hazel |

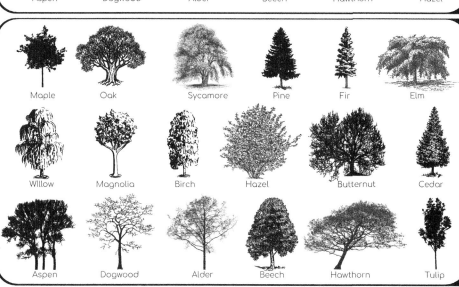

| | | | | | |
|---|---|---|---|---|---|
| Maple | Oak | Sycamore | Pine | Fir | Elm |
| Wlllow | Magnolia | Birch | Hazel | Butternut | Cedar |
| Aspen | Dogwood | Alder | Beech | Hawthorn | Tulip |

_____
_____
_____
_____
_____
_____
_____
_____
_____
_____

## Environment

Location / GPS: _____  Date _____

Season:  ○ Spring  ○ Summer  ○ Fall  ○ Winter

Surroundings:  ○ Hedgerows  ○ Field  ○ Park  ○ Woodland  ○ Water
○ Other _____

Setting:  ○ Natural  ○ Artificial    **Type:**  ○ Evergreen  ○ Deciduous

Notes: _____

_____

## General

Shape:  ○ Vase  ○ Columnar  ○ Round  ○ (Other) _____

Features:  ○ Conical/Spire  ○ Spreading  ○ Upright  ○ Weeping
○ (Other) _____

Branching:  ○ Opposite  ○ Alternate    **Estimated Age:** _____

Notes: _____

_____

## Needles or Leaves

Type:  ○ Needle  ○ Simple Broadleaf  ○ Compound Broadleaf  ○ Scales

Shape:  ○ Cordate (heart-shaped)  ○ Lanceolate (long and narrow)
○ Deltoid (triangular)  ○ Obicular (round)  ○ Ovate (egg-shaped)
○ Palm and Maple  ○ Lobed

Structure:  ○ Simple (attached to twigs or twig stems)
○ Compound (attached to single lead steam)

Notes: _____

_____

## Flowers, Fruits & Seeds

Flower Type:  ○ Single Blooms  ○ Clustered Blooms  ○ Catkins

Fruits / Seeds:  ○ Berries  ○ Apples  ○ Pears  ○ Nuts  ○ Acorns
○ Cones  ○ Capsules  ○ Catkins  ○ (Other) _____

Notes: _____

_____

## Leaf Buds & Twigs

Bud Type:  ○ Terminal (grows at tip of a shoot causing shoot to grow longer)
○ Lateral (grow along sides of a shoot causing sideways growth)

Twig Features:  ○ Smooth  ○ Hairy  ○ Spines  ○ Corky Ribs
○ (Other) _____

Notes: _____

## Bark

Texture:  ○ Furrowed  ○ Scaly  ○ Peeling  ○ Smooth  ○ Shiny
○ Fissured  ○ Ridges / Depressions  ○ Papery  ○ Warty
○ (Other) _____

Color:  ○ Gray  ○ Brown  ○ Cinnamon  ○ White  ○ Silver
○ Green  ○ Copper  ○ (Other) _____

Notes: _____

Maple    Oak    Sycamore    Pine    Fir    Elm

Wlllow    Magnolia    Birch    Tulip    Butternut    Cedar

Aspen    Dogwood    Alder    Beech    Hawthorn    Hazel

Maple    Oak    Sycamore    Pine    Fir    Elm

Wlllow    Magnolia    Birch    Hazel    Butternut    Cedar

Aspen    Dogwood    Alder    Beech    Hawthorn    Tulip

## Environment

Location / GPS: _____  Date _____

Season: ○ Spring  ○ Summer  ○ Fall  ○ Winter

Surroundings: ○ Hedgerows  ○ Field  ○ Park  ○ Woodland  ○ Water
○ Other _____

Setting: ○ Natural  ○ Artificial  **Type:** ○ Evergreen  ○ Deciduous

Notes: _____
_____
_____

## General

Shape: ○ Vase  ○ Columnar  ○ Round  ○ (Other) _____

Features: ○ Conical/Spire  ○ Spreading  ○ Upright  ○ Weeping
○ (Other) _____

Branching: ○ Opposite  ○ Alternate  **Estimated Age:** _____

Notes: _____
_____
_____

## Needles or Leaves

Type: ○ Needle  ○ Simple Broadleaf  ○ Compound Broadleaf  ○ Scales

Shape: ○ Cordate (heart-shaped)  ○ Lanceolate (long and narrow)
○ Deltoid (triangular)  ○ Obicular (round)  ○ Ovate (egg-shaped)
○ Palm and Maple  ○ Lobed

Structure: ○ Simple (attached to twigs or twig stems)
○ Compound (attached to single lead steam)

Notes: _____
_____
_____

## Flowers, Fruits & Seeds

Flower Type: ○ Single Blooms  ○ Clustered Blooms  ○ Catkins

Fruits / Seeds: ○ Berries  ○ Apples  ○ Pears  ○ Nuts  ○ Acorns
○ Cones  ○ Capsules  ○ Catkins  ○ (Other) _____

Notes: _____
_____
_____

## Leaf Buds & Twigs

Bud Type: ○ Terminal (grows at tip of a shoot causing shoot to grow longer)
○ Lateral (grow along sides of a shoot causing sideways growth)

Twig Features: ○ Smooth  ○ Hairy  ○ Spines  ○ Corky Ribs
○ (Other) _____

Notes: _____

## Bark

Texture: ○ Furrowed  ○ Scaly  ○ Peeling  ○ Smooth  ○ Shiny
○ Fissured  ○ Ridges / Depressions  ○ Papery  ○ Warty
○ (Other) _____

Color: ○ Gray  ○ Brown  ○ Cinnamon  ○ White  ○ Silver
○ Green  ○ Copper  ○ (Other) _____

Notes: _____

Maple · Oak · Sycamore · Pine · Fir · Elm

Willow · Magnolia · Birch · Tulip · Butternut · Cedar

Aspen · Dogwood · Alder · Beech · Hawthorn · Hazel

Maple · Oak · Sycamore · Pine · Fir · Elm

Willow · Magnolia · Birch · Hazel · Butternut · Cedar

Aspen · Dogwood · Alder · Beech · Hawthorn · Tulip

## Environment

Location / GPS: _____ Date _____

Season: ○ Spring ○ Summer ○ Fall ○ Winter

Surroundings: ○ Hedgerows ○ Field ○ Park ○ Woodland ○ Water
○ Other_____

Setting: ○ Natural ○ Artificial    Type: ○ Evergreen ○ Deciduous

Notes: _____
_____

## General

Shape: ○ Vase ○ Columnar ○ Round ○ (Other) _____

Features: ○ Conical/Spire ○ Spreading ○ Upright ○ Weeping
○ (Other) _____

Branching: ○ Opposite ○ Alternate    Estimated Age: _____

Notes: _____
_____

## Needles or Leaves

Type: ○ Needle ○ Simple Broadleaf ○ Compound Broadleaf ○ Scales

Shape: ○ Cordate (heart-shaped) ○ Lanceolate (long and narrow)
○ Deltoid (triangular) ○ Obicular (round) ○ Ovate (egg-shaped)
○ Palm and Maple ○ Lobed

Structure: ○ Simple (attached to twigs or twig stems)
○ Compound (attached to single lead steam)

Notes: _____
_____

## Flowers, Fruits & Seeds

Flower Type: ○ Single Blooms ○ Clustered Blooms ○ Catkins

Fruits / Seeds: ○ Berries ○ Apples ○ Pears ○ Nuts ○ Acorns
○ Cones ○ Capsules ○ Catkins ○ (Other) _____

Notes: _____
_____

## Leaf Buds & Twigs

Bud Type: ○ Terminal (grows at tip of a shoot causing shoot to grow longer)
○ Lateral (grow along sides of a shoot causing sideways growth)

Twig Features: ○ Smooth ○ Hairy ○ Spines ○ Corky Ribs
○ (Other) _____

Notes: _____

## Bark

Texture: ○ Furrowed ○ Scaly ○ Peeling ○ Smooth ○ Shiny
○ Fissured ○ Ridges / Depressions ○ Papery ○ Warty
○ (Other) _____

Color: ○ Gray ○ Brown ○ Cinnamon ○ White ○ Silver
○ Green ○ Copper ○ (Other) _____

Notes: _____

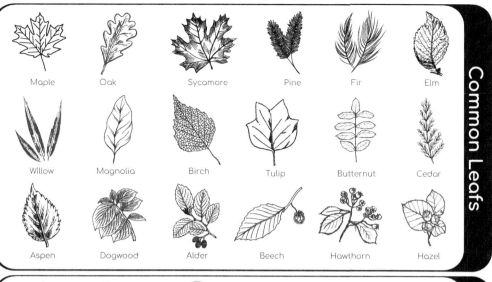

Maple | Oak | Sycamore | Pine | Fir | Elm
Wlllow | Magnolia | Birch | Tulip | Butternut | Cedar
Aspen | Dogwood | Alder | Beech | Hawthorn | Hazel

Maple | Oak | Sycamore | Pine | Fir | Elm
Wlllow | Magnolia | Birch | Hazel | Butternut | Cedar
Aspen | Dogwood | Alder | Beech | Hawthorn | Tulip

## Environment

Location / GPS: _____ Date _____

Season: ○ Spring ○ Summer ○ Fall ○ Winter

Surroundings: ○ Hedgerows ○ Field ○ Park ○ Woodland ○ Water
○ Other _____

Setting: ○ Natural ○ Artificial   Type: ○ Evergreen ○ Deciduous

Notes: _____
_____

## General

Shape: ○ Vase ○ Columnar ○ Round ○ (Other) _____

Features: ○ Conical/Spire ○ Spreading ○ Upright ○ Weeping
○ (Other) _____

Branching: ○ Opposite ○ Alternate   Estimated Age: _____

Notes: _____
_____

## Needles or Leaves

Type: ○ Needle ○ Simple Broadleaf ○ Compound Broadleaf ○ Scales

Shape: ○ Cordate (heart-shaped) ○ Lanceolate (long and narrow)
○ Deltoid (triangular) ○ Obicular (round) ○ Ovate (egg-shaped)
○ Palm and Maple ○ Lobed

Structure: ○ Simple (attached to twigs or twig stems)
○ Compound (attached to single lead steam)

Notes: _____
_____

## Flowers, Fruits & Seeds

Flower Type: ○ Single Blooms ○ Clustered Blooms ○ Catkins

Fruits / Seeds: ○ Berries ○ Apples ○ Pears ○ Nuts ○ Acorns
○ Cones ○ Capsules ○ Catkins ○ (Other) _____

Notes: _____
_____

## Leaf Buds & Twigs

Bud Type: ○ Terminal (grows at tip of a shoot causing shoot to grow longer)
○ Lateral (grow along sides of a shoot causing sideways growth)

Twig Features: ○ Smooth ○ Hairy ○ Spines ○ Corky Ribs
○ (Other) _____

Notes: _____

## Bark

Texture: ○ Furrowed ○ Scaly ○ Peeling ○ Smooth ○ Shiny
○ Fissured ○ Ridges / Depressions ○ Papery ○ Warty
○ (Other) _____

Color: ○ Gray ○ Brown ○ Cinnamon ○ White ○ Silver
○ Green ○ Copper ○ (Other) _____

Notes: _____

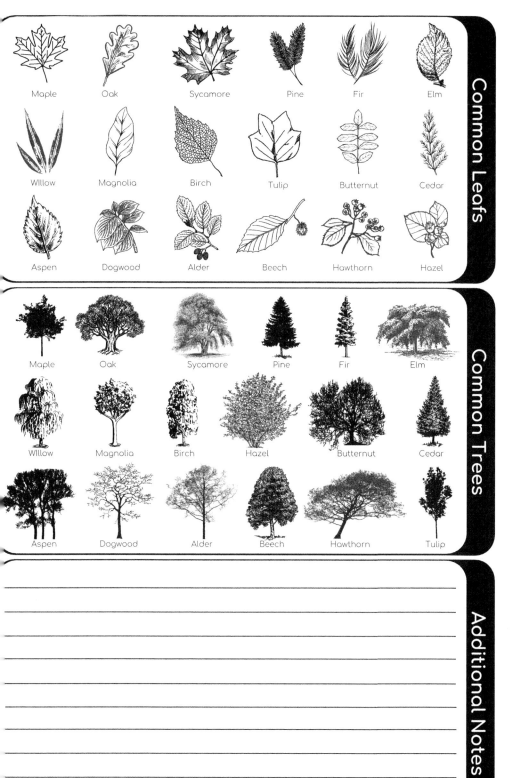

| | | | | | |
|---|---|---|---|---|---|
| Maple | Oak | Sycamore | Pine | Fir | Elm |
| WIllow | Magnolia | Birch | Tulip | Butternut | Cedar |
| Aspen | Dogwood | Alder | Beech | Hawthorn | Hazel |

| | | | | | |
|---|---|---|---|---|---|
| Maple | Oak | Sycamore | Pine | Fir | Elm |
| WIllow | Magnolia | Birch | Hazel | Butternut | Cedar |
| Aspen | Dogwood | Alder | Beech | Hawthorn | Tulip |

## Environment

Location / GPS: _____  Date _____

Season:  ○ Spring  ○ Summer  ○ Fall  ○ Winter

Surroundings:  ○ Hedgerows  ○ Field  ○ Park  ○ Woodland  ○ Water
○ Other _____

Setting:  ○ Natural  ○ Artificial    **Type:**  ○ Evergreen  ○ Deciduous

Notes: _____
_____
_____

## General

Shape:  ○ Vase  ○ Columnar  ○ Round  ○ (Other) _____

Features:  ○ Conical/Spire  ○ Spreading  ○ Upright  ○ Weeping
○ (Other) _____

Branching:  ○ Opposite  ○ Alternate    **Estimated Age:** _____

Notes: _____
_____
_____

## Needles or Leaves

Type:  ○ Needle  ○ Simple Broadleaf  ○ Compound Broadleaf  ○ Scales

Shape:  ○ Cordate (heart-shaped)  ○ Lanceolate (long and narrow)
○ Deltoid (triangular)  ○ Obicular (round)  ○ Ovate (egg-shaped)
○ Palm and Maple  ○ Lobed

Structure:  ○ Simple (attached to twigs or twig stems)
○ Compound (attached to single lead steam)

Notes: _____
_____
_____

## Flowers, Fruits & Seeds

Flower Type:  ○ Single Blooms  ○ Clustered Blooms  ○ Catkins

Fruits / Seeds:  ○ Berries  ○ Apples  ○ Pears  ○ Nuts  ○ Acorns
○ Cones  ○ Capsules  ○ Catkins  ○ (Other) _____

Notes: _____
_____
_____

## Leaf Buds & Twigs

Bud Type:  ○ Terminal (grows at tip of a shoot causing shoot to grow longer)
○ Lateral (grow along sides of a shoot causing sideways growth)

Twig Features:  ○ Smooth  ○ Hairy  ○ Spines  ○ Corky Ribs
○ (Other) _____

Notes: _____

## Bark

Texture:  ○ Furrowed  ○ Scaly  ○ Peeling  ○ Smooth  ○ Shiny
○ Fissured  ○ Ridges / Depressions  ○ Papery  ○ Warty
○ (Other) _____

Color:  ○ Gray  ○ Brown  ○ Cinnamon  ○ White  ○ Silver
○ Green  ○ Copper  ○ (Other) _____

Notes: _____

Maple    Oak    Sycamore    Pine    Fir    Elm

WIllow    Magnolia    Birch    Tulip    Butternut    Cedar

Aspen    Dogwood    Alder    Beech    Hawthorn    Hazel

Maple    Oak    Sycamore    Pine    Fir    Elm

WIllow    Magnolia    Birch    Hazel    Butternut    Cedar

Aspen    Dogwood    Alder    Beech    Hawthorn    Tulip

## Environment

Location / GPS: _____ Date _____

Season: ◯ Spring  ◯ Summer  ◯ Fall  ◯ Winter

Surroundings: ◯ Hedgerows  ◯ Field  ◯ Park  ◯ Woodland  ◯ Water
◯ Other_____

Setting: ◯ Natural  ◯ Artificial   Type: ◯ Evergreen  ◯ Deciduous

Notes: _____
_____

## General

Shape: ◯ Vase  ◯ Columnar  ◯ Round  ◯ (Other) _____

Features: ◯ Conical/Spire  ◯ Spreading  ◯ Upright  ◯ Weeping
◯ (Other) _____

Branching: ◯ Opposite  ◯ Alternate   Estimated Age: _____

Notes: _____
_____

## Needles or Leaves

Type: ◯ Needle  ◯ Simple Broadleaf  ◯ Compound Broadleaf  ◯ Scales

Shape: ◯ Cordate (heart-shaped)  ◯ Lanceolate (long and narrow)
◯ Deltoid (triangular)  ◯ Obicular (round)  ◯ Ovate (egg-shaped)
◯ Palm and Maple  ◯ Lobed

Structure: ◯ Simple (attached to twigs or twig stems)
◯ Compound (attached to single lead steam)

Notes: _____
_____

## Flowers, Fruits & Seeds

Flower Type: ◯ Single Blooms  ◯ Clustered Blooms  ◯ Catkins

Fruits / Seeds: ◯ Berries  ◯ Apples  ◯ Pears  ◯ Nuts  ◯ Acorns
◯ Cones  ◯ Capsules  ◯ Catkins  ◯ (Other) _____

Notes: _____
_____

## Leaf Buds & Twigs

Bud Type: ◯ Terminal (grows at tip of a shoot causing shoot to grow longer)
◯ Lateral (grow along sides of a shoot causing sideways growth)

Twig Features: ◯ Smooth  ◯ Hairy  ◯ Spines  ◯ Corky Ribs
◯ (Other) _____

Notes: _____

## Bark

Texture: ◯ Furrowed  ◯ Scaly  ◯ Peeling  ◯ Smooth  ◯ Shiny
◯ Fissured  ◯ Ridges / Depressions  ◯ Papery  ◯ Warty
◯ (Other) _____

Color: ◯ Gray  ◯ Brown  ◯ Cinnamon  ◯ White  ◯ Silver
◯ Green  ◯ Copper  ◯ (Other) _____

Notes: _____

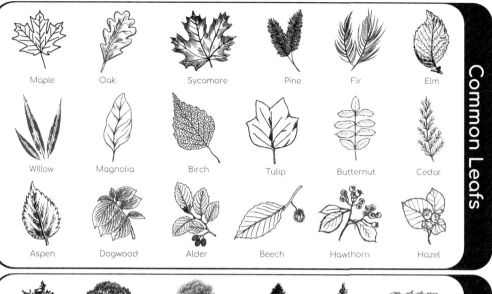

Maple    Oak    Sycamore    Pine    Fir    Elm

WIllow    Magnolia    Birch    Tulip    Butternut    Cedar

Aspen    Dogwood    Alder    Beech    Hawthorn    Hazel

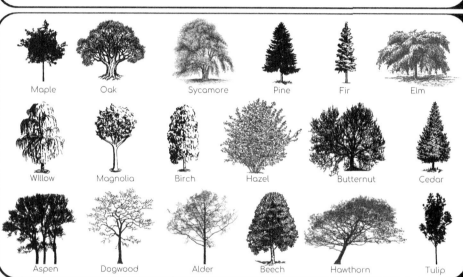

Maple    Oak    Sycamore    Pine    Fir    Elm

WIllow    Magnolia    Birch    Hazel    Butternut    Cedar

Aspen    Dogwood    Alder    Beech    Hawthorn    Tulip

## Environment

Location / GPS: _____     Date _____

Season:  ○ Spring     ○ Summer     ○ Fall     ○ Winter

Surroundings:  ○ Hedgerows  ○ Field  ○ Park  ○ Woodland  ○ Water
○ Other_____

Setting:  ○ Natural  ○ Artificial     Type:  ○ Evergreen  ○ Deciduous

Notes:_____
_____

## General

Shape:  ○ Vase  ○ Columnar  ○ Round  ○ (Other) _____

Features:  ○ Conical/Spire  ○ Spreading  ○ Upright  ○ Weeping
○ (Other) _____

Branching:  ○ Opposite  ○ Alternate     Estimated Age: _____

Notes: _____
_____

## Needles or Leaves

Type:  ○ Needle  ○ Simple Broadleaf  ○ Compound Broadleaf  ○ Scales

Shape:  ○ Cordate (heart-shaped)  ○ Lanceolate (long and narrow)
○ Deltoid (triangular)  ○ Obicular (round)  ○ Ovate (egg-shaped)
○ Palm and Maple  ○ Lobed

Structure:  ○ Simple (attached to twigs or twig stems)
○ Compound (attached to single lead steam)

Notes: _____
_____

## Flowers, Fruits & Seeds

Flower Type:  ○ Single Blooms  ○ Clustered Blooms  ○ Catkins

Fruits / Seeds:  ○ Berries  ○ Apples  ○ Pears  ○ Nuts  ○ Acorns
○ Cones  ○ Capsules  ○ Catkins  ○ (Other) _____

Notes: _____
_____

## Leaf Buds & Twigs

Bud Type:  ○ Terminal (grows at tip of a shoot causing shoot to grow longer)
○ Lateral (grow along sides of a shoot causing sideways growth)

Twig Features:  ○ Smooth  ○ Hairy  ○ Spines  ○ Corky Ribs
○ (Other) _____

Notes: _____

## Bark

Texture:  ○ Furrowed  ○ Scaly  ○ Peeling  ○ Smooth  ○ Shiny
○ Fissured  ○ Ridges / Depressions  ○ Papery  ○ Warty
○ (Other) _____

Color:  ○ Gray  ○ Brown  ○ Cinnamon  ○ White  ○ Silver
○ Green  ○ Copper  ○ (Other) _____

Notes: _____

| | | | | | |
|---|---|---|---|---|---|
| Maple | Oak | Sycamore | Pine | Fir | Elm |
| WIllow | Magnolia | Birch | Tulip | Butternut | Cedar |
| Aspen | Dogwood | Alder | Beech | Hawthorn | Hazel |

| | | | | | |
|---|---|---|---|---|---|
| Maple | Oak | Sycamore | Pine | Fir | Elm |
| WIllow | Magnolia | Birch | Hazel | Butternut | Cedar |
| Aspen | Dogwood | Alder | Beech | Hawthorn | Tulip |

## Environment

Location / GPS: _____ Date _____

Season: ◯ Spring ◯ Summer ◯ Fall ◯ Winter

Surroundings: ◯ Hedgerows ◯ Field ◯ Park ◯ Woodland ◯ Water
◯ Other _____

Setting: ◯ Natural ◯ Artificial **Type:** ◯ Evergreen ◯ Deciduous

Notes: _____
_____

## General

Shape: ◯ Vase ◯ Columnar ◯ Round ◯ (Other) _____

Features: ◯ Conical/Spire ◯ Spreading ◯ Upright ◯ Weeping
◯ (Other) _____

Branching: ◯ Opposite ◯ Alternate **Estimated Age:** _____

Notes: _____
_____

## Needles or Leaves

Type: ◯ Needle ◯ Simple Broadleaf ◯ Compound Broadleaf ◯ Scales

Shape: ◯ Cordate (heart-shaped) ◯ Lanceolate (long and narrow)
◯ Deltoid (triangular) ◯ Obicular (round) ◯ Ovate (egg-shaped)
◯ Palm and Maple ◯ Lobed

Structure: ◯ Simple (attached to twigs or twig stems)
◯ Compound (attached to single lead steam)

Notes: _____
_____

## Flowers, Fruits & Seeds

Flower Type: ◯ Single Blooms ◯ Clustered Blooms ◯ Catkins

Fruits / Seeds: ◯ Berries ◯ Apples ◯ Pears ◯ Nuts ◯ Acorns
◯ Cones ◯ Capsules ◯ Catkins ◯ (Other) _____

Notes: _____
_____

## Leaf Buds & Twigs

Bud Type: ◯ Terminal (grows at tip of a shoot causing shoot to grow longer)
◯ Lateral (grow along sides of a shoot causing sideways growth)

Twig Features: ◯ Smooth ◯ Hairy ◯ Spines ◯ Corky Ribs
◯ (Other) _____

Notes: _____

## Bark

Texture: ◯ Furrowed ◯ Scaly ◯ Peeling ◯ Smooth ◯ Shiny
◯ Fissured ◯ Ridges / Depressions ◯ Papery ◯ Warty
◯ (Other) _____

Color: ◯ Gray ◯ Brown ◯ Cinnamon ◯ White ◯ Silver
◯ Green ◯ Copper ◯ (Other) _____

Notes: _____

Maple

Oak

Sycamore

Pine

Fir

Elm

Wlllow

Magnolia

Birch

Tulip

Butternut

Cedar

Aspen

Dogwood

Alder

Beech

Hawthorn

Hazel

Maple

Oak

Sycamore

Pine

Fir

Elm

Wlllow

Magnolia

Birch

Hazel

Butternut

Cedar

Aspen

Dogwood

Alder

Beech

Hawthorn

Tulip

## Environment

Location / GPS: _____ Date _____

Season: ○ Spring ○ Summer ○ Fall ○ Winter

Surroundings: ○ Hedgerows ○ Field ○ Park ○ Woodland ○ Water
○ Other _____

Setting: ○ Natural ○ Artificial   Type: ○ Evergreen ○ Deciduous

Notes: _____
_____

## General

Shape: ○ Vase ○ Columnar ○ Round ○ (Other) _____

Features: ○ Conical/Spire ○ Spreading ○ Upright ○ Weeping
○ (Other) _____

Branching: ○ Opposite ○ Alternate   Estimated Age: _____

Notes: _____
_____

## Needles or Leaves

Type: ○ Needle ○ Simple Broadleaf ○ Compound Broadleaf ○ Scales

Shape: ○ Cordate (heart-shaped) ○ Lanceolate (long and narrow)
○ Deltoid (triangular) ○ Obicular (round) ○ Ovate (egg-shaped)
○ Palm and Maple ○ Lobed

Structure: ○ Simple (attached to twigs or twig stems)
○ Compound (attached to single lead steam)

Notes: _____
_____

## Flowers, Fruits & Seeds

Flower Type: ○ Single Blooms ○ Clustered Blooms ○ Catkins

Fruits / Seeds: ○ Berries ○ Apples ○ Pears ○ Nuts ○ Acorns
○ Cones ○ Capsules ○ Catkins ○ (Other) _____

Notes: _____
_____

## Leaf Buds & Twigs

Bud Type: ○ Terminal (grows at tip of a shoot causing shoot to grow longer)
○ Lateral (grow along sides of a shoot causing sideways growth)

Twig Features: ○ Smooth ○ Hairy ○ Spines ○ Corky Ribs
○ (Other) _____

Notes: _____

## Bark

Texture: ○ Furrowed ○ Scaly ○ Peeling ○ Smooth ○ Shiny
○ Fissured ○ Ridges / Depressions ○ Papery ○ Warty
○ (Other) _____

Color: ○ Gray ○ Brown ○ Cinnamon ○ White ○ Silver
○ Green ○ Copper ○ (Other) _____

Notes: _____

## Common Leafs

| | | | | | |
|---|---|---|---|---|---|
| Maple | Oak | Sycamore | Pine | Fir | Elm |
| WIllow | Magnolia | Birch | Tulip | Butternut | Cedar |
| Aspen | Dogwood | Alder | Beech | Hawthorn | Hazel |

## Common Trees

| | | | | | |
|---|---|---|---|---|---|
| Maple | Oak | Sycamore | Pine | Fir | Elm |
| WIllow | Magnolia | Birch | Hazel | Butternut | Cedar |
| Aspen | Dogwood | Alder | Beech | Hawthorn | Tulip |

## Additional Notes

## Environment

Location / GPS: _____ Date _____

Season: ○ Spring ○ Summer ○ Fall ○ Winter

Surroundings: ○ Hedgerows ○ Field ○ Park ○ Woodland ○ Water
○ Other _____

Setting: ○ Natural ○ Artificial    Type: ○ Evergreen ○ Deciduous

Notes: _____

_____

## General

Shape: ○ Vase ○ Columnar ○ Round ○ (Other) _____

Features: ○ Conical/Spire ○ Spreading ○ Upright ○ Weeping
○ (Other) _____

Branching: ○ Opposite ○ Alternate    Estimated Age: _____

Notes: _____

_____

## Needles or Leaves

Type: ○ Needle ○ Simple Broadleaf ○ Compound Broadleaf ○ Scales

Shape: ○ Cordate (heart-shaped) ○ Lanceolate (long and narrow)
○ Deltoid (triangular) ○ Obicular (round) ○ Ovate (egg-shaped)
○ Palm and Maple ○ Lobed

Structure: ○ Simple (attached to twigs or twig stems)
○ Compound (attached to single lead steam)

Notes: _____

_____

## Flowers, Fruits & Seeds

Flower Type: ○ Single Blooms ○ Clustered Blooms ○ Catkins

Fruits / Seeds: ○ Berries ○ Apples ○ Pears ○ Nuts ○ Acorns
○ Cones ○ Capsules ○ Catkins ○ (Other) _____

Notes: _____

_____

## Leaf Buds & Twigs

Bud Type: ○ Terminal (grows at tip of a shoot causing shoot to grow longer)
○ Lateral (grow along sides of a shoot causing sideways growth)

Twig Features: ○ Smooth ○ Hairy ○ Spines ○ Corky Ribs
○ (Other) _____

Notes: _____

## Bark

Texture: ○ Furrowed ○ Scaly ○ Peeling ○ Smooth ○ Shiny
○ Fissured ○ Ridges / Depressions ○ Papery ○ Warty
○ (Other) _____

Color: ○ Gray ○ Brown ○ Cinnamon ○ White ○ Silver
○ Green ○ Copper ○ (Other) _____

Notes: _____

| | | | | | |
|---|---|---|---|---|---|
| Maple | Oak | Sycamore | Pine | Fir | Elm |
| Wlllow | Magnolia | Birch | Tulip | Butternut | Cedar |
| Aspen | Dogwood | Alder | Beech | Hawthorn | Hazel |

| | | | | | |
|---|---|---|---|---|---|
| Maple | Oak | Sycamore | Pine | Fir | Elm |
| Wlllow | Magnolia | Birch | Hazel | Butternut | Cedar |
| Aspen | Dogwood | Alder | Beech | Hawthorn | Tulip |

## Environment

Location / GPS: _____  Date _____

Season: ○ Spring ○ Summer ○ Fall ○ Winter

Surroundings: ○ Hedgerows ○ Field ○ Park ○ Woodland ○ Water
○ Other _____

Setting: ○ Natural ○ Artificial   Type: ○ Evergreen ○ Deciduous

Notes: _____
_____

## General

Shape: ○ Vase ○ Columnar ○ Round ○ (Other) _____

Features: ○ Conical/Spire ○ Spreading ○ Upright ○ Weeping
○ (Other) _____

Branching: ○ Opposite ○ Alternate   Estimated Age: _____

Notes: _____
_____

## Needles or Leaves

Type: ○ Needle ○ Simple Broadleaf ○ Compound Broadleaf ○ Scales

Shape: ○ Cordate (heart-shaped) ○ Lanceolate (long and narrow)
○ Deltoid (triangular) ○ Obicular (round) ○ Ovate (egg-shaped)
○ Palm and Maple ○ Lobed

Structure: ○ Simple (attached to twigs or twig stems)
○ Compound (attached to single lead steam)

Notes: _____
_____

## Flowers, Fruits & Seeds

Flower Type: ○ Single Blooms ○ Clustered Blooms ○ Catkins

Fruits / Seeds: ○ Berries ○ Apples ○ Pears ○ Nuts ○ Acorns
○ Cones ○ Capsules ○ Catkins ○ (Other) _____

Notes: _____
_____

## Leaf Buds & Twigs

Bud Type: ○ Terminal (grows at tip of a shoot causing shoot to grow longer)
○ Lateral (grow along sides of a shoot causing sideways growth)

Twig Features: ○ Smooth ○ Hairy ○ Spines ○ Corky Ribs
○ (Other) _____

Notes: _____

## Bark

Texture: ○ Furrowed ○ Scaly ○ Peeling ○ Smooth ○ Shiny
○ Fissured ○ Ridges / Depressions ○ Papery ○ Warty
○ (Other) _____

Color: ○ Gray ○ Brown ○ Cinnamon ○ White ○ Silver
○ Green ○ Copper ○ (Other) _____

Notes: _____

Maple · Oak · Sycamore · Pine · Fir · Elm

Willow · Magnolia · Birch · Tulip · Butternut · Cedar

Aspen · Dogwood · Alder · Beech · Hawthorn · Hazel

Maple · Oak · Sycamore · Pine · Fir · Elm

Willow · Magnolia · Birch · Hazel · Butternut · Cedar

Aspen · Dogwood · Alder · Beech · Hawthorn · Tulip

## Environment

Location / GPS: _____ Date _____

Season: ◯ Spring ◯ Summer ◯ Fall ◯ Winter

Surroundings: ◯ Hedgerows ◯ Field ◯ Park ◯ Woodland ◯ Water
◯ Other _____

Setting: ◯ Natural ◯ Artificial     Type: ◯ Evergreen ◯ Deciduous

Notes: _____
_____
_____

## General

Shape: ◯ Vase ◯ Columnar ◯ Round ◯ (Other) _____

Features: ◯ Conical/Spire ◯ Spreading ◯ Upright ◯ Weeping
◯ (Other) _____

Branching: ◯ Opposite ◯ Alternate     Estimated Age: _____

Notes: _____
_____
_____

## Needles or Leaves

Type: ◯ Needle ◯ Simple Broadleaf ◯ Compound Broadleaf ◯ Scales

Shape: ◯ Cordate (heart-shaped) ◯ Lanceolate (long and narrow)
◯ Deltoid (triangular) ◯ Obicular (round) ◯ Ovate (egg-shaped)
◯ Palm and Maple ◯ Lobed

Structure: ◯ Simple (attached to twigs or twig stems)
◯ Compound (attached to single lead steam)

Notes: _____
_____
_____

## Flowers, Fruits & Seeds

Flower Type: ◯ Single Blooms ◯ Clustered Blooms ◯ Catkins

Fruits / Seeds: ◯ Berries ◯ Apples ◯ Pears ◯ Nuts ◯ Acorns
◯ Cones ◯ Capsules ◯ Catkins ◯ (Other) _____

Notes: _____
_____
_____

## Leaf Buds & Twigs

Bud Type: ◯ Terminal (grows at tip of a shoot causing shoot to grow longer)
◯ Lateral (grow along sides of a shoot causing sideways growth)

Twig Features: ◯ Smooth ◯ Hairy ◯ Spines ◯ Corky Ribs
◯ (Other) _____

Notes: _____
_____

## Bark

Texture: ◯ Furrowed ◯ Scaly ◯ Peeling ◯ Smooth ◯ Shiny
◯ Fissured ◯ Ridges / Depressions ◯ Papery ◯ Warty
◯ (Other) _____

Color: ◯ Gray ◯ Brown ◯ Cinnamon ◯ White ◯ Silver
◯ Green ◯ Copper ◯ (Other) _____

Notes: _____

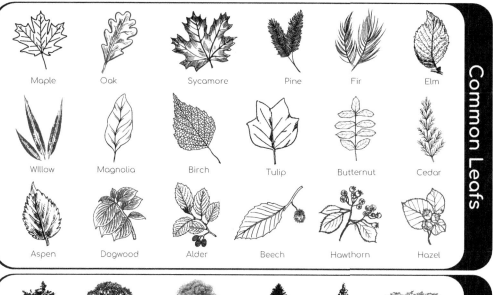

## Environment

Location / GPS: _____ Date _____

Season: ○ Spring ○ Summer ○ Fall ○ Winter

Surroundings: ○ Hedgerows ○ Field ○ Park ○ Woodland ○ Water
○ Other _____

Setting: ○ Natural ○ Artificial     Type: ○ Evergreen ○ Deciduous

Notes: _____
_____

## General

Shape: ○ Vase ○ Columnar ○ Round ○ (Other) _____

Features: ○ Conical/Spire ○ Spreading ○ Upright ○ Weeping
○ (Other) _____

Branching: ○ Opposite ○ Alternate     Estimated Age: _____

Notes: _____
_____

## Needles or Leaves

Type: ○ Needle ○ Simple Broadleaf ○ Compound Broadleaf ○ Scales

Shape: ○ Cordate (heart-shaped) ○ Lanceolate (long and narrow)
○ Deltoid (triangular) ○ Obicular (round) ○ Ovate (egg-shaped)
○ Palm and Maple ○ Lobed

Structure: ○ Simple (attached to twigs or twig stems)
○ Compound (attached to single lead steam)

Notes: _____
_____

## Flowers, Fruits & Seeds

Flower Type: ○ Single Blooms ○ Clustered Blooms ○ Catkins

Fruits / Seeds: ○ Berries ○ Apples ○ Pears ○ Nuts ○ Acorns
○ Cones ○ Capsules ○ Catkins ○ (Other) _____

Notes: _____
_____

## Leaf Buds & Twigs

Bud Type: ○ Terminal (grows at tip of a shoot causing shoot to grow longer)
○ Lateral (grow along sides of a shoot causing sideways growth)

Twig Features: ○ Smooth ○ Hairy ○ Spines ○ Corky Ribs
○ (Other) _____

Notes: _____

## Bark

Texture: ○ Furrowed ○ Scaly ○ Peeling ○ Smooth ○ Shiny
○ Fissured ○ Ridges / Depressions ○ Papery ○ Warty
○ (Other) _____

Color: ○ Gray ○ Brown ○ Cinnamon ○ White ○ Silver
○ Green ○ Copper ○ (Other) _____

Notes: _____

Maple  Oak  Sycamore  Pine  Fir  Elm

WIllow  Magnolia  Birch  Tulip  Butternut  Cedar

Aspen  Dogwood  Alder  Beech  Hawthorn  Hazel

Maple  Oak  Sycamore  Pine  Fir  Elm

WIllow  Magnolia  Birch  Hazel  Butternut  Cedar

Aspen  Dogwood  Alder  Beech  Hawthorn  Tulip

## Environment

Location / GPS: _____ Date _____

Season: ○ Spring  ○ Summer  ○ Fall  ○ Winter

Surroundings: ○ Hedgerows  ○ Field  ○ Park  ○ Woodland  ○ Water
○ Other_____

Setting: ○ Natural  ○ Artificial  **Type:** ○ Evergreen  ○ Deciduous

Notes: _____
_____
_____

## General

Shape: ○ Vase  ○ Columnar  ○ Round  ○ (Other) _____

Features: ○ Conical/Spire  ○ Spreading  ○ Upright  ○ Weeping
○ (Other) _____

Branching: ○ Opposite  ○ Alternate  **Estimated Age:** _____

Notes: _____
_____
_____

## Needles or Leaves

Type: ○ Needle  ○ Simple Broadleaf  ○ Compound Broadleaf  ○ Scales

Shape: ○ Cordate (heart-shaped)  ○ Lanceolate (long and narrow)
○ Deltoid (triangular)  ○ Obicular (round)  ○ Ovate (egg-shaped)
○ Palm and Maple  ○ Lobed

Structure: ○ Simple (attached to twigs or twig stems)
○ Compound (attached to single lead steam)

Notes: _____
_____
_____

## Flowers, Fruits & Seeds

Flower Type: ○ Single Blooms  ○ Clustered Blooms  ○ Catkins

Fruits / Seeds: ○ Berries  ○ Apples  ○ Pears  ○ Nuts  ○ Acorns
○ Cones  ○ Capsules  ○ Catkins  ○ (Other) _____

Notes: _____
_____
_____

## Leaf Buds & Twigs

Bud Type: ○ Terminal (grows at tip of a shoot causing shoot to grow longer)
○ Lateral (grow along sides of a shoot causing sideways growth)

Twig Features: ○ Smooth  ○ Hairy  ○ Spines  ○ Corky Ribs
○ (Other) _____

Notes: _____

## Bark

Texture: ○ Furrowed  ○ Scaly  ○ Peeling  ○ Smooth  ○ Shiny
○ Fissured  ○ Ridges / Depressions  ○ Papery  ○ Warty
○ (Other) _____

Color: ○ Gray  ○ Brown  ○ Cinnamon  ○ White  ○ Silver
○ Green  ○ Copper  ○ (Other) _____

Notes: _____

Maple  Oak  Sycamore  Pine  Fir  Elm

Wlllow  Magnolia  Birch  Tulip  Butternut  Cedar

Aspen  Dogwood  Alder  Beech  Hawthorn  Hazel

Maple  Oak  Sycamore  Pine  Fir  Elm

Wlllow  Magnolia  Birch  Hazel  Butternut  Cedar

Aspen  Dogwood  Alder  Beech  Hawthorn  Tulip

## Environment

Location / GPS: _____ Date _____

Season: ○ Spring ○ Summer ○ Fall ○ Winter

Surroundings: ○ Hedgerows ○ Field ○ Park ○ Woodland ○ Water
○ Other _____

Setting: ○ Natural ○ Artificial    Type: ○ Evergreen ○ Deciduous

Notes: _____
_____

## General

Shape: ○ Vase ○ Columnar ○ Round ○ (Other) _____

Features: ○ Conical/Spire ○ Spreading ○ Upright ○ Weeping
○ (Other) _____

Branching: ○ Opposite ○ Alternate    Estimated Age: _____

Notes: _____
_____

## Needles or Leaves

Type: ○ Needle ○ Simple Broadleaf ○ Compound Broadleaf ○ Scales

Shape: ○ Cordate (heart-shaped) ○ Lanceolate (long and narrow)
○ Deltoid (triangular) ○ Obicular (round) ○ Ovate (egg-shaped)
○ Palm and Maple ○ Lobed

Structure: ○ Simple (attached to twigs or twig stems)
○ Compound (attached to single lead steam)

Notes: _____
_____

## Flowers, Fruits & Seeds

Flower Type: ○ Single Blooms ○ Clustered Blooms ○ Catkins

Fruits / Seeds: ○ Berries ○ Apples ○ Pears ○ Nuts ○ Acorns
○ Cones ○ Capsules ○ Catkins ○ (Other) _____

Notes: _____
_____

## Leaf Buds & Twigs

Bud Type: ○ Terminal (grows at tip of a shoot causing shoot to grow longer)
○ Lateral (grow along sides of a shoot causing sideways growth)

Twig Features: ○ Smooth ○ Hairy ○ Spines ○ Corky Ribs
○ (Other) _____

Notes: _____

## Bark

Texture: ○ Furrowed ○ Scaly ○ Peeling ○ Smooth ○ Shiny
○ Fissured ○ Ridges / Depressions ○ Papery ○ Warty
○ (Other) _____

Color: ○ Gray ○ Brown ○ Cinnamon ○ White ○ Silver
○ Green ○ Copper ○ (Other) _____

Notes: _____

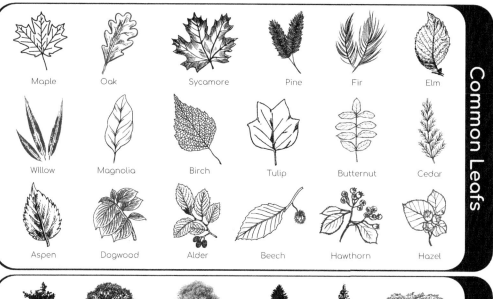

Maple  Oak  Sycamore  Pine  Fir  Elm

Wlllow  Magnolia  Birch  Tulip  Butternut  Cedar

Aspen  Dogwood  Alder  Beech  Hawthorn  Hazel

Maple  Oak  Sycamore  Pine  Fir  Elm

Wlllow  Magnolia  Birch  Hazel  Butternut  Cedar

Aspen  Dogwood  Alder  Beech  Hawthorn  Tulip

## Environment

Location / GPS: _____ Date _____

Season: ○ Spring ○ Summer ○ Fall ○ Winter

Surroundings: ○ Hedgerows ○ Field ○ Park ○ Woodland ○ Water
○ Other _____

Setting: ○ Natural ○ Artificial     Type: ○ Evergreen ○ Deciduous

Notes: _____
_____

## General

Shape: ○ Vase ○ Columnar ○ Round ○ (Other) _____

Features: ○ Conical/Spire ○ Spreading ○ Upright ○ Weeping
○ (Other) _____

Branching: ○ Opposite ○ Alternate     Estimated Age: _____

Notes: _____
_____

## Needles or Leaves

Type: ○ Needle ○ Simple Broadleaf ○ Compound Broadleaf ○ Scales

Shape: ○ Cordate (heart-shaped) ○ Lanceolate (long and narrow)
○ Deltoid (triangular) ○ Obicular (round) ○ Ovate (egg-shaped)
○ Palm and Maple ○ Lobed

Structure: ○ Simple (attached to twigs or twig stems)
○ Compound (attached to single lead steam)

Notes: _____
_____

## Flowers, Fruits & Seeds

Flower Type: ○ Single Blooms ○ Clustered Blooms ○ Catkins

Fruits / Seeds: ○ Berries ○ Apples ○ Pears ○ Nuts ○ Acorns
○ Cones ○ Capsules ○ Catkins ○ (Other) _____

Notes: _____
_____

## Leaf Buds & Twigs

Bud Type: ○ Terminal (grows at tip of a shoot causing shoot to grow longer)
○ Lateral (grow along sides of a shoot causing sideways growth)

Twig Features: ○ Smooth ○ Hairy ○ Spines ○ Corky Ribs
○ (Other) _____

Notes: _____

## Bark

Texture: ○ Furrowed ○ Scaly ○ Peeling ○ Smooth ○ Shiny
○ Fissured ○ Ridges / Depressions ○ Papery ○ Warty
○ (Other) _____

Color: ○ Gray ○ Brown ○ Cinnamon ○ White ○ Silver
○ Green ○ Copper ○ (Other) _____

Notes: _____

Maple  Oak  Sycamore  Pine  Fir  Elm

Wlllow  Magnolia  Birch  Tulip  Butternut  Cedar

Aspen  Dogwood  Alder  Beech  Hawthorn  Hazel

Maple  Oak  Sycamore  Pine  Fir  Elm

Wlllow  Magnolia  Birch  Hazel  Butternut  Cedar

Aspen  Dogwood  Alder  Beech  Hawthorn  Tulip

## Environment

Location / GPS: _____ Date _____

Season: ○ Spring   ○ Summer   ○ Fall   ○ Winter

Surroundings: ○ Hedgerows  ○ Field  ○ Park  ○ Woodland  ○ Water
○ Other_____

Setting: ○ Natural  ○ Artificial   **Type:** ○ Evergreen   ○ Deciduous

Notes: _____
_____
_____

## General

Shape: ○ Vase  ○ Columnar  ○ Round  ○ (Other) _____

Features: ○ Conical/Spire  ○ Spreading  ○ Upright  ○ Weeping
○ (Other) _____

Branching: ○ Opposite  ○ Alternate   **Estimated Age:** _____

Notes: _____
_____
_____

## Needles or Leaves

Type: ○ Needle  ○ Simple Broadleaf  ○ Compound Broadleaf  ○ Scales

Shape: ○ Cordate (heart-shaped)  ○ Lanceolate (long and narrow)
○ Deltoid (triangular)  ○ Obicular (round)  ○ Ovate (egg-shaped)
○ Palm and Maple  ○ Lobed

Structure: ○ Simple (attached to twigs or twig stems)
○ Compound (attached to single lead steam)

Notes: _____
_____
_____

## Flowers, Fruits & Seeds

Flower Type: ○ Single Blooms  ○ Clustered Blooms  ○ Catkins

Fruits / Seeds: ○ Berries  ○ Apples  ○ Pears  ○ Nuts  ○ Acorns
○ Cones  ○ Capsules  ○ Catkins  ○ (Other) _____

Notes: _____
_____
_____

## Leaf Buds & Twigs

Bud Type: ○ Terminal (grows at tip of a shoot causing shoot to grow longer)
○ Lateral (grow along sides of a shoot causing sideways growth)

Twig Features: ○ Smooth  ○ Hairy  ○ Spines  ○ Corky Ribs
○ (Other) _____

Notes: _____

## Bark

Texture: ○ Furrowed  ○ Scaly  ○ Peeling  ○ Smooth  ○ Shiny
○ Fissured  ○ Ridges / Depressions  ○ Papery  ○ Warty
○ (Other) _____

Color: ○ Gray  ○ Brown  ○ Cinnamon  ○ White  ○ Silver
○ Green  ○ Copper  ○ (Other) _____

Notes: _____

Maple  Oak  Sycamore  Pine  Fir  Elm

Willow  Magnolia  Birch  Tulip  Butternut  Cedar

Aspen  Dogwood  Alder  Beech  Hawthorn  Hazel

Maple  Oak  Sycamore  Pine  Fir  Elm

Willow  Magnolia  Birch  Hazel  Butternut  Cedar

Aspen  Dogwood  Alder  Beech  Hawthorn  Tulip

## Environment

Location / GPS: _____  Date _____

Season:  ○ Spring  ○ Summer  ○ Fall  ○ Winter

Surroundings:  ○ Hedgerows  ○ Field  ○ Park  ○ Woodland  ○ Water
  ○ Other_____

Setting:  ○ Natural  ○ Artificial  **Type:** ○ Evergreen  ○ Deciduous

Notes: _____
_____
_____

## General

Shape:  ○ Vase  ○ Columnar  ○ Round  ○ (Other) _____

Features:  ○ Conical/Spire  ○ Spreading  ○ Upright  ○ Weeping
  ○ (Other) _____

Branching:  ○ Opposite  ○ Alternate  **Estimated Age:** _____

Notes: _____
_____
_____

## Needles or Leaves

Type:  ○ Needle  ○ Simple Broadleaf  ○ Compound Broadleaf  ○ Scales

Shape:  ○ Cordate (heart-shaped)  ○ Lanceolate (long and narrow)
  ○ Deltoid (triangular)  ○ Obicular (round)  ○ Ovate (egg-shaped)
  ○ Palm and Maple  ○ Lobed

Structure:  ○ Simple (attached to twigs or twig stems)
  ○ Compound (attached to single lead steam)

Notes: _____
_____
_____

## Flowers, Fruits & Seeds

Flower Type:  ○ Single Blooms  ○ Clustered Blooms  ○ Catkins

Fruits / Seeds:  ○ Berries  ○ Apples  ○ Pears  ○ Nuts  ○ Acorns
  ○ Cones  ○ Capsules  ○ Catkins  ○ (Other) _____

Notes: _____
_____
_____

## Leaf Buds & Twigs

Bud Type:  ○ Terminal (grows at tip of a shoot causing shoot to grow longer)
  ○ Lateral (grow along sides of a shoot causing sideways growth)

Twig Features:  ○ Smooth  ○ Hairy  ○ Spines  ○ Corky Ribs
  ○ (Other) _____

Notes: _____

## Bark

Texture:  ○ Furrowed  ○ Scaly  ○ Peeling  ○ Smooth  ○ Shiny
  ○ Fissured  ○ Ridges / Depressions  ○ Papery  ○ Warty
  ○ (Other) _____

Color:  ○ Gray  ○ Brown  ○ Cinnamon  ○ White  ○ Silver
  ○ Green  ○ Copper  ○ (Other) _____

Notes: _____

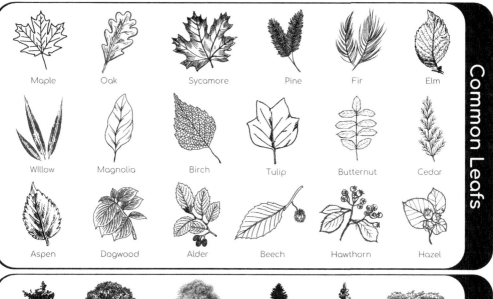

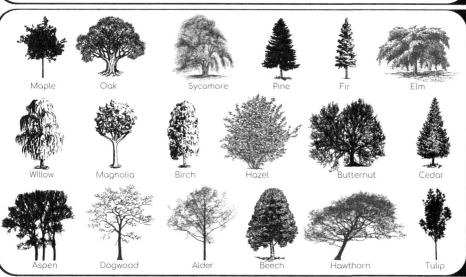

## Environment

Location / GPS: _____ Date _____

Season: ◯ Spring ◯ Summer ◯ Fall ◯ Winter

Surroundings: ◯ Hedgerows ◯ Field ◯ Park ◯ Woodland ◯ Water
◯ Other _____

Setting: ◯ Natural ◯ Artificial    Type: ◯ Evergreen ◯ Deciduous

Notes: _____
_____

## General

Shape: ◯ Vase ◯ Columnar ◯ Round ◯ (Other) _____

Features: ◯ Conical/Spire ◯ Spreading ◯ Upright ◯ Weeping
◯ (Other) _____

Branching: ◯ Opposite ◯ Alternate    Estimated Age: _____

Notes: _____
_____

## Needles or Leaves

Type: ◯ Needle ◯ Simple Broadleaf ◯ Compound Broadleaf ◯ Scales

Shape: ◯ Cordate (heart-shaped) ◯ Lanceolate (long and narrow)
◯ Deltoid (triangular) ◯ Obicular (round) ◯ Ovate (egg-shaped)
◯ Palm and Maple ◯ Lobed

Structure: ◯ Simple (attached to twigs or twig stems)
◯ Compound (attached to single lead steam)

Notes: _____
_____

## Flowers, Fruits & Seeds

Flower Type: ◯ Single Blooms ◯ Clustered Blooms ◯ Catkins

Fruits / Seeds: ◯ Berries ◯ Apples ◯ Pears ◯ Nuts ◯ Acorns
◯ Cones ◯ Capsules ◯ Catkins ◯ (Other) _____

Notes: _____
_____

## Leaf Buds & Twigs

Bud Type: ◯ Terminal (grows at tip of a shoot causing shoot to grow longer)
◯ Lateral (grow along sides of a shoot causing sideways growth)

Twig Features: ◯ Smooth ◯ Hairy ◯ Spines ◯ Corky Ribs
◯ (Other) _____

Notes: _____

## Bark

Texture: ◯ Furrowed ◯ Scaly ◯ Peeling ◯ Smooth ◯ Shiny
◯ Fissured ◯ Ridges / Depressions ◯ Papery ◯ Warty
◯ (Other) _____

Color: ◯ Gray ◯ Brown ◯ Cinnamon ◯ White ◯ Silver
◯ Green ◯ Copper ◯ (Other) _____

Notes: _____

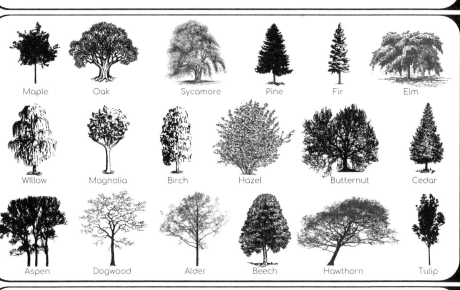

| | | | | | |
|---|---|---|---|---|---|
| Maple | Oak | Sycamore | Pine | Fir | Elm |
| Willow | Magnolia | Birch | Tulip | Butternut | Cedar |
| Aspen | Dogwood | Alder | Beech | Hawthorn | Hazel |

| | | | | | |
|---|---|---|---|---|---|
| Maple | Oak | Sycamore | Pine | Fir | Elm |
| Willow | Magnolia | Birch | Hazel | Butternut | Cedar |
| Aspen | Dogwood | Alder | Beech | Hawthorn | Tulip |

## Environment

Location / GPS: _____ Date _____

Season: ○ Spring  ○ Summer  ○ Fall  ○ Winter

Surroundings: ○ Hedgerows  ○ Field  ○ Park  ○ Woodland  ○ Water
○ Other _____

Setting: ○ Natural  ○ Artificial    Type: ○ Evergreen  ○ Deciduous

Notes: _____
_____
_____

## General

Shape: ○ Vase  ○ Columnar  ○ Round  ○ (Other) _____

Features: ○ Conical/Spire  ○ Spreading  ○ Upright  ○ Weeping
○ (Other) _____

Branching: ○ Opposite  ○ Alternate    Estimated Age: _____

Notes: _____
_____
_____

## Needles or Leaves

Type: ○ Needle  ○ Simple Broadleaf  ○ Compound Broadleaf  ○ Scales

Shape: ○ Cordate (heart-shaped)  ○ Lanceolate (long and narrow)
○ Deltoid (triangular)  ○ Obicular (round)  ○ Ovate (egg-shaped)
○ Palm and Maple  ○ Lobed

Structure: ○ Simple (attached to twigs or twig stems)
○ Compound (attached to single lead steam)

Notes: _____
_____
_____

## Flowers, Fruits & Seeds

Flower Type: ○ Single Blooms  ○ Clustered Blooms  ○ Catkins

Fruits / Seeds: ○ Berries  ○ Apples  ○ Pears  ○ Nuts  ○ Acorns
○ Cones  ○ Capsules  ○ Catkins  ○ (Other) _____

Notes: _____
_____
_____

## Leaf Buds & Twigs

Bud Type: ○ Terminal (grows at tip of a shoot causing shoot to grow longer)
○ Lateral (grow along sides of a shoot causing sideways growth)

Twig Features: ○ Smooth  ○ Hairy  ○ Spines  ○ Corky Ribs
○ (Other) _____

Notes: _____

## Bark

Texture: ○ Furrowed  ○ Scaly  ○ Peeling  ○ Smooth  ○ Shiny
○ Fissured  ○ Ridges / Depressions  ○ Papery  ○ Warty
○ (Other) _____

Color: ○ Gray  ○ Brown  ○ Cinnamon  ○ White  ○ Silver
○ Green  ○ Copper  ○ (Other) _____

Notes: _____

Maple  Oak  Sycamore  Pine  Fir  Elm

Willow  Magnolia  Birch  Tulip  Butternut  Cedar

Aspen  Dogwood  Alder  Beech  Hawthorn  Hazel

Maple  Oak  Sycamore  Pine  Fir  Elm

Willow  Magnolia  Birch  Hazel  Butternut  Cedar

Aspen  Dogwood  Alder  Beech  Hawthorn  Tulip

## Environment

Location / GPS: _____  Date _____

Season: ○ Spring   ○ Summer   ○ Fall   ○ Winter

Surroundings: ○ Hedgerows   ○ Field   ○ Park   ○ Woodland   ○ Water
              ○ Other _____

Setting: ○ Natural   ○ Artificial   **Type:** ○ Evergreen   ○ Deciduous

Notes: _____
       _____

## General

Shape: ○ Vase   ○ Columnar   ○ Round   ○ (Other) _____

Features: ○ Conical/Spire   ○ Spreading   ○ Upright   ○ Weeping
          ○ (Other) _____

Branching: ○ Opposite   ○ Alternate   **Estimated Age:** _____

Notes: _____
       _____

## Needles or Leaves

Type: ○ Needle   ○ Simple Broadleaf   ○ Compound Broadleaf   ○ Scales

Shape: ○ Cordate (heart-shaped)   ○ Lanceolate (long and narrow)
       ○ Deltoid (triangular)   ○ Obicular (round)   ○ Ovate (egg-shaped)
       ○ Palm and Maple   ○ Lobed

Structure: ○ Simple (attached to twigs or twig stems)
           ○ Compound (attached to single lead steam)

Notes: _____
       _____

## Flowers, Fruits & Seeds

Flower Type: ○ Single Blooms   ○ Clustered Blooms   ○ Catkins

Fruits / Seeds: ○ Berries   ○ Apples   ○ Pears   ○ Nuts   ○ Acorns
                ○ Cones   ○ Capsules   ○ Catkins   ○ (Other) _____

Notes: _____
       _____

## Leaf Buds & Twigs

Bud Type: ○ Terminal (grows at tip of a shoot causing shoot to grow longer)
          ○ Lateral (grow along sides of a shoot causing sideways growth)

Twig Features: ○ Smooth   ○ Hairy   ○ Spines   ○ Corky Ribs
               ○ (Other) _____

Notes: _____

## Bark

Texture: ○ Furrowed   ○ Scaly   ○ Peeling   ○ Smooth   ○ Shiny
         ○ Fissured   ○ Ridges / Depressions   ○ Papery   ○ Warty
         ○ (Other) _____

Color: ○ Gray   ○ Brown   ○ Cinnamon   ○ White   ○ Silver
       ○ Green   ○ Copper   ○ (Other) _____

Notes: _____

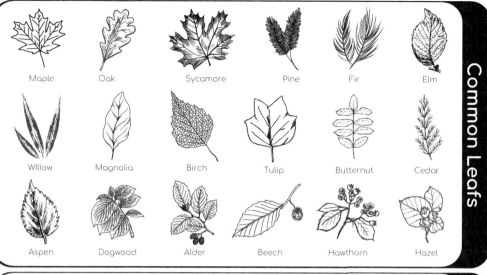

Maple | Oak | Sycamore | Pine | Fir | Elm
Wlllow | Magnolia | Birch | Tulip | Butternut | Cedar
Aspen | Dogwood | Alder | Beech | Hawthorn | Hazel

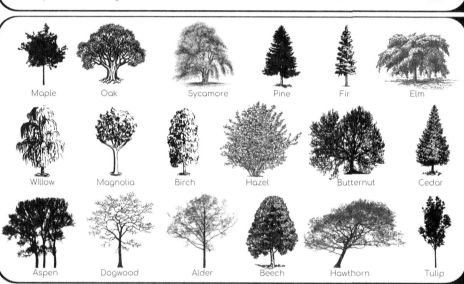

Maple | Oak | Sycamore | Pine | Fir | Elm
Wlllow | Magnolia | Birch | Hazel | Butternut | Cedar
Aspen | Dogwood | Alder | Beech | Hawthorn | Tulip

## Environment

Location / GPS: _____ Date _____

Season: ◯ Spring ◯ Summer ◯ Fall ◯ Winter

Surroundings: ◯ Hedgerows ◯ Field ◯ Park ◯ Woodland ◯ Water
◯ Other _____

Setting: ◯ Natural ◯ Artificial Type: ◯ Evergreen ◯ Deciduous

Notes: _____
_____

## General

Shape: ◯ Vase ◯ Columnar ◯ Round ◯ (Other) _____

Features: ◯ Conical/Spire ◯ Spreading ◯ Upright ◯ Weeping
◯ (Other) _____

Branching: ◯ Opposite ◯ Alternate Estimated Age: _____

Notes: _____
_____

## Needles or Leaves

Type: ◯ Needle ◯ Simple Broadleaf ◯ Compound Broadleaf ◯ Scales

Shape: ◯ Cordate (heart-shaped) ◯ Lanceolate (long and narrow)
◯ Deltoid (triangular) ◯ Obicular (round) ◯ Ovate (egg-shaped)
◯ Palm and Maple ◯ Lobed

Structure: ◯ Simple (attached to twigs or twig stems)
◯ Compound (attached to single lead steam)

Notes: _____
_____

## Flowers, Fruits & Seeds

Flower Type: ◯ Single Blooms ◯ Clustered Blooms ◯ Catkins

Fruits / Seeds: ◯ Berries ◯ Apples ◯ Pears ◯ Nuts ◯ Acorns
◯ Cones ◯ Capsules ◯ Catkins ◯ (Other) _____

Notes: _____
_____

## Leaf Buds & Twigs

Bud Type: ◯ Terminal (grows at tip of a shoot causing shoot to grow longer)
◯ Lateral (grow along sides of a shoot causing sideways growth)

Twig Features: ◯ Smooth ◯ Hairy ◯ Spines ◯ Corky Ribs
◯ (Other) _____

Notes: _____

## Bark

Texture: ◯ Furrowed ◯ Scaly ◯ Peeling ◯ Smooth ◯ Shiny
◯ Fissured ◯ Ridges / Depressions ◯ Papery ◯ Warty
◯ (Other) _____

Color: ◯ Gray ◯ Brown ◯ Cinnamon ◯ White ◯ Silver
◯ Green ◯ Copper ◯ (Other) _____

Notes: _____

Maple  Oak  Sycamore  Pine  Fir  Elm

Wlllow  Magnolia  Birch  Tulip  Butternut  Cedar

Aspen  Dogwood  Alder  Beech  Hawthorn  Hazel

Maple  Oak  Sycamore  Pine  Fir  Elm

Wlllow  Magnolia  Birch  Hazel  Butternut  Cedar

Aspen  Dogwood  Alder  Beech  Hawthorn  Tulip

## Environment

Location / GPS: _____  Date _____

Season:  ○ Spring   ○ Summer   ○ Fall   ○ Winter

Surroundings:  ○ Hedgerows  ○ Field  ○ Park  ○ Woodland  ○ Water
○ Other _____

Setting:  ○ Natural  ○ Artificial    Type:  ○ Evergreen   ○ Deciduous

Notes: _____
_____
_____

## General

Shape:  ○ Vase  ○ Columnar  ○ Round  ○(Other) _____

Features:  ○ Conical/Spire  ○ Spreading  ○ Upright  ○ Weeping
○(Other) _____

Branching:  ○ Opposite  ○ Alternate    Estimated Age: _____

Notes: _____
_____
_____

## Needles or Leaves

Type:  ○ Needle  ○ Simple Broadleaf  ○ Compound Broadleaf  ○ Scales

Shape:  ○ Cordate (heart-shaped)  ○ Lanceolate (long and narrow)
○ Deltoid (triangular)  ○ Obicular (round)  ○ Ovate (egg-shaped)
○ Palm and Maple  ○ Lobed

Structure:  ○ Simple (attached to twigs or twig stems)
○ Compound (attached to single lead steam)

Notes: _____
_____
_____

## Flowers, Fruits & Seeds

Flower Type:  ○ Single Blooms  ○ Clustered Blooms  ○ Catkins

Fruits / Seeds:  ○ Berries  ○ Apples  ○ Pears  ○ Nuts  ○ Acorns
○ Cones  ○ Capsules  ○ Catkins  ○(Other) _____

Notes: _____
_____
_____

## Leaf Buds & Twigs

Bud Type:  ○ Terminal (grows at tip of a shoot causing shoot to grow longer)
○ Lateral (grow along sides of a shoot causing sideways growth)

Twig Features:  ○ Smooth  ○ Hairy  ○ Spines  ○ Corky Ribs
○(Other) _____

Notes: _____

## Bark

Texture:  ○ Furrowed  ○ Scaly  ○ Peeling  ○ Smooth  ○ Shiny
○ Fissured  ○ Ridges / Depressions  ○ Papery  ○ Warty
○(Other) _____

Color:  ○ Gray  ○ Brown  ○ Cinnamon  ○ White  ○ Silver
○ Green  ○ Copper  ○(Other) _____

Notes: _____

| | | | | | |
|---|---|---|---|---|---|
| Maple | Oak | Sycamore | Pine | Fir | Elm |
| WIllow | Magnolia | Birch | Tulip | Butternut | Cedar |
| Aspen | Dogwood | Alder | Beech | Hawthorn | Hazel |

| | | | | | |
|---|---|---|---|---|---|
| Maple | Oak | Sycamore | Pine | Fir | Elm |
| WIllow | Magnolia | Birch | Hazel | Butternut | Cedar |
| Aspen | Dogwood | Alder | Beech | Hawthorn | Tulip |

## Environment

Location / GPS: _____ Date _____

Season: ○ Spring  ○ Summer  ○ Fall  ○ Winter

Surroundings: ○ Hedgerows  ○ Field  ○ Park  ○ Woodland  ○ Water
○ Other_____

Setting: ○ Natural  ○ Artificial    Type: ○ Evergreen  ○ Deciduous

Notes:_____
_____
_____

## General

Shape: ○ Vase  ○ Columnar  ○ Round  ○ (Other) _____

Features: ○ Conical/Spire  ○ Spreading  ○ Upright  ○ Weeping
○ (Other) _____

Branching: ○ Opposite  ○ Alternate    Estimated Age: _____

Notes: _____
_____
_____

## Needles or Leaves

Type: ○ Needle  ○ Simple Broadleaf  ○ Compound Broadleaf  ○ Scales

Shape: ○ Cordate (heart-shaped)  ○ Lanceolate (long and narrow)
○ Deltoid (triangular)  ○ Obicular (round)  ○ Ovate (egg-shaped)
○ Palm and Maple  ○ Lobed

Structure: ○ Simple (attached to twigs or twig stems)
○ Compound (attached to single lead steam)

Notes: _____
_____
_____

## Flowers, Fruits & Seeds

Flower Type: ○ Single Blooms  ○ Clustered Blooms  ○ Catkins

Fruits / Seeds: ○ Berries  ○ Apples  ○ Pears  ○ Nuts  ○ Acorns
○ Cones  ○ Capsules  ○ Catkins  ○ (Other) _____

Notes: _____
_____
_____

## Leaf Buds & Twigs

Bud Type: ○ Terminal (grows at tip of a shoot causing shoot to grow longer)
○ Lateral (grow along sides of a shoot causing sideways growth)

Twig Features: ○ Smooth  ○ Hairy  ○ Spines  ○ Corky Ribs
○ (Other) _____

Notes: _____
_____

## Bark

Texture: ○ Furrowed  ○ Scaly  ○ Peeling  ○ Smooth  ○ Shiny
○ Fissured  ○ Ridges / Depressions  ○ Papery  ○ Warty
○ (Other) _____

Color: ○ Gray  ○ Brown  ○ Cinnamon  ○ White  ○ Silver
○ Green  ○ Copper  ○ (Other) _____

Notes: _____

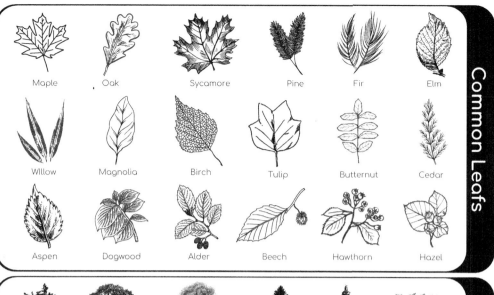

Maple · Oak · Sycamore · Pine · Fir · Elm

Willow · Magnolia · Birch · Tulip · Butternut · Cedar

Aspen · Dogwood · Alder · Beech · Hawthorn · Hazel

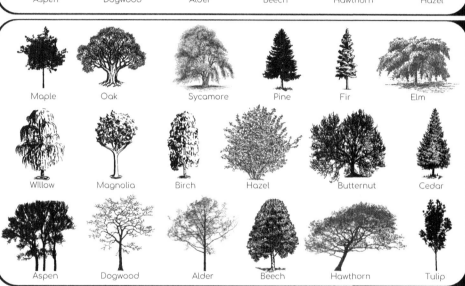

Maple · Oak · Sycamore · Pine · Fir · Elm

Willow · Magnolia · Birch · Hazel · Butternut · Cedar

Aspen · Dogwood · Alder · Beech · Hawthorn · Tulip

## Environment

Location / GPS: _____  Date _____

Season: ○ Spring  ○ Summer  ○ Fall  ○ Winter

Surroundings: ○ Hedgerows  ○ Field  ○ Park  ○ Woodland  ○ Water
○ Other_____

Setting: ○ Natural  ○ Artificial  **Type:** ○ Evergreen  ○ Deciduous

Notes: _____
_____

## General

Shape: ○ Vase  ○ Columnar  ○ Round  ○ (Other) _____

Features: ○ Conical/Spire  ○ Spreading  ○ Upright  ○ Weeping
○ (Other) _____

Branching: ○ Opposite  ○ Alternate  **Estimated Age:** _____

Notes: _____
_____

## Needles or Leaves

Type: ○ Needle  ○ Simple Broadleaf  ○ Compound Broadleaf  ○ Scales

Shape: ○ Cordate (heart-shaped)  ○ Lanceolate (long and narrow)
○ Deltoid (triangular)  ○ Obicular (round)  ○ Ovate (egg-shaped)
○ Palm and Maple  ○ Lobed

Structure: ○ Simple (attached to twigs or twig stems)
○ Compound (attached to single lead steam)

Notes: _____
_____

## Flowers, Fruits & Seeds

Flower Type: ○ Single Blooms  ○ Clustered Blooms  ○ Catkins

Fruits / Seeds: ○ Berries  ○ Apples  ○ Pears  ○ Nuts  ○ Acorns
○ Cones  ○ Capsules  ○ Catkins  ○ (Other) _____

Notes: _____
_____

## Leaf Buds & Twigs

Bud Type: ○ Terminal (grows at tip of a shoot causing shoot to grow longer)
○ Lateral (grow along sides of a shoot causing sideways growth)

Twig Features: ○ Smooth  ○ Hairy  ○ Spines  ○ Corky Ribs
○ (Other) _____

Notes: _____

## Bark

Texture: ○ Furrowed  ○ Scaly  ○ Peeling  ○ Smooth  ○ Shiny
○ Fissured  ○ Ridges / Depressions  ○ Papery  ○ Warty
○ (Other) _____

Color: ○ Gray  ○ Brown  ○ Cinnamon  ○ White  ○ Silver
○ Green  ○ Copper  ○ (Other) _____

Notes: _____

Maple  Oak  Sycamore  Pine  Fir  Elm

Wlllow  Magnolia  Birch  Tulip  Butternut  Cedar

Aspen  Dogwood  Alder  Beech  Hawthorn  Hazel

Maple  Oak  Sycamore  Pine  Fir  Elm

Wlllow  Magnolia  Birch  Hazel  Butternut  Cedar

Aspen  Dogwood  Alder  Beech  Hawthorn  Tulip

## Environment

Location / GPS: _____ Date _____

Season: ○ Spring  ○ Summer  ○ Fall  ○ Winter

Surroundings: ○ Hedgerows  ○ Field  ○ Park  ○ Woodland  ○ Water
○ Other _____

Setting: ○ Natural  ○ Artificial    Type: ○ Evergreen  ○ Deciduous

Notes: _____
_____
_____

## General

Shape: ○ Vase  ○ Columnar  ○ Round  ○ (Other) _____

Features: ○ Conical/Spire  ○ Spreading  ○ Upright  ○ Weeping
○ (Other) _____

Branching: ○ Opposite  ○ Alternate    Estimated Age: _____

Notes: _____
_____
_____

## Needles or Leaves

Type: ○ Needle  ○ Simple Broadleaf  ○ Compound Broadleaf  ○ Scales

Shape: ○ Cordate (heart-shaped)   ○ Lanceolate (long and narrow)
○ Deltoid (triangular)  ○ Obicular (round)  ○ Ovate (egg-shaped)
○ Palm and Maple  ○ Lobed

Structure: ○ Simple (attached to twigs or twig stems)
○ Compound (attached to single lead steam)

Notes: _____
_____
_____

## Flowers, Fruits & Seeds

Flower Type: ○ Single Blooms  ○ Clustered Blooms  ○ Catkins

Fruits / Seeds: ○ Berries  ○ Apples  ○ Pears  ○ Nuts  ○ Acorns
○ Cones  ○ Capsules  ○ Catkins  ○ (Other) _____

Notes: _____
_____
_____

## Leaf Buds & Twigs

Bud Type: ○ Terminal (grows at tip of a shoot causing shoot to grow longer)
○ Lateral (grow along sides of a shoot causing sideways growth)

Twig Features: ○ Smooth  ○ Hairy  ○ Spines  ○ Corky Ribs
○ (Other) _____

Notes: _____

## Bark

Texture: ○ Furrowed  ○ Scaly  ○ Peeling  ○ Smooth  ○ Shiny
○ Fissured  ○ Ridges / Depressions  ○ Papery  ○ Warty
○ (Other) _____

Color: ○ Gray  ○ Brown  ○ Cinnamon  ○ White  ○ Silver
○ Green  ○ Copper  ○ (Other) _____

Notes: _____

Maple Oak Sycamore Pine Fir Elm

Wlllow Magnolia Birch Tulip Butternut Cedar

Aspen Dogwood Alder Beech Hawthorn Hazel

Maple Oak Sycamore Pine Fir Elm

Wlllow Magnolia Birch Hazel Butternut Cedar

Aspen Dogwood Alder Beech Hawthorn Tulip

## Environment

Location / GPS: _____ Date _____

Season: ◯ Spring ◯ Summer ◯ Fall ◯ Winter

Surroundings: ◯ Hedgerows ◯ Field ◯ Park ◯ Woodland ◯ Water
◯ Other _____

Setting: ◯ Natural ◯ Artificial  Type: ◯ Evergreen ◯ Deciduous

Notes: _____
_____

## General

Shape: ◯ Vase ◯ Columnar ◯ Round ◯ (Other) _____

Features: ◯ Conical/Spire ◯ Spreading ◯ Upright ◯ Weeping
◯ (Other) _____

Branching: ◯ Opposite ◯ Alternate  Estimated Age: _____

Notes: _____
_____

## Needles or Leaves

Type: ◯ Needle ◯ Simple Broadleaf ◯ Compound Broadleaf ◯ Scales

Shape: ◯ Cordate (heart-shaped) ◯ Lanceolate (long and narrow)
◯ Deltoid (triangular) ◯ Obicular (round) ◯ Ovate (egg-shaped)
◯ Palm and Maple ◯ Lobed

Structure: ◯ Simple (attached to twigs or twig stems)
◯ Compound (attached to single lead steam)

Notes: _____
_____

## Flowers, Fruits & Seeds

Flower Type: ◯ Single Blooms ◯ Clustered Blooms ◯ Catkins

Fruits / Seeds: ◯ Berries ◯ Apples ◯ Pears ◯ Nuts ◯ Acorns
◯ Cones ◯ Capsules ◯ Catkins ◯ (Other) _____

Notes: _____
_____

## Leaf Buds & Twigs

Bud Type: ◯ Terminal (grows at tip of a shoot causing shoot to grow longer)
◯ Lateral (grow along sides of a shoot causing sideways growth)

Twig Features: ◯ Smooth ◯ Hairy ◯ Spines ◯ Corky Ribs
◯ (Other) _____

Notes: _____

## Bark

Texture: ◯ Furrowed ◯ Scaly ◯ Peeling ◯ Smooth ◯ Shiny
◯ Fissured ◯ Ridges / Depressions ◯ Papery ◯ Warty
◯ (Other) _____

Color: ◯ Gray ◯ Brown ◯ Cinnamon ◯ White ◯ Silver
◯ Green ◯ Copper ◯ (Other) _____

Notes: _____

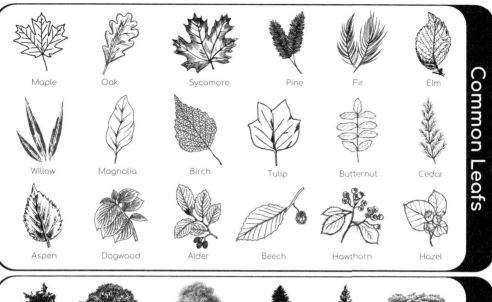

Maple   Oak   Sycamore   Pine   Fir   Elm

Wlllow   Magnolia   Birch   Tulip   Butternut   Cedar

Aspen   Dogwood   Alder   Beech   Hawthorn   Hazel

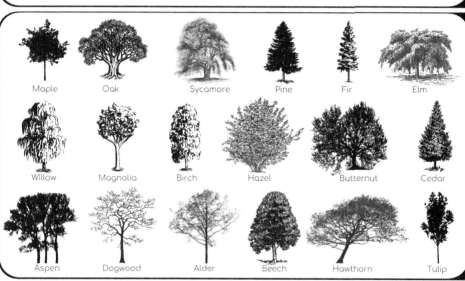

Maple   Oak   Sycamore   Pine   Fir   Elm

Wlllow   Magnolia   Birch   Hazel   Butternut   Cedar

Aspen   Dogwood   Alder   Beech   Hawthorn   Tulip

## Environment

Location / GPS: _____ Date _____

Season: ○ Spring  ○ Summer  ○ Fall  ○ Winter

Surroundings: ○ Hedgerows  ○ Field  ○ Park  ○ Woodland  ○ Water
○ Other_____

Setting: ○ Natural  ○ Artificial  **Type:** ○ Evergreen  ○ Deciduous

Notes: _____
_____

## General

Shape: ○ Vase  ○ Columnar  ○ Round  ○ (Other) _____

Features: ○ Conical/Spire  ○ Spreading  ○ Upright  ○ Weeping
○ (Other) _____

Branching: ○ Opposite  ○ Alternate  **Estimated Age:** _____

Notes: _____
_____

## Needles or Leaves

Type: ○ Needle  ○ Simple Broadleaf  ○ Compound Broadleaf  ○ Scales

Shape: ○ Cordate (heart-shaped)  ○ Lanceolate (long and narrow)
○ Deltoid (triangular)  ○ Obicular (round)  ○ Ovate (egg-shaped)
○ Palm and Maple  ○ Lobed

Structure: ○ Simple (attached to twigs or twig stems)
○ Compound (attached to single lead steam)

Notes: _____
_____

## Flowers, Fruits & Seeds

Flower Type: ○ Single Blooms  ○ Clustered Blooms  ○ Catkins

Fruits / Seeds: ○ Berries  ○ Apples  ○ Pears  ○ Nuts  ○ Acorns
○ Cones  ○ Capsules  ○ Catkins  ○ (Other) _____

Notes: _____
_____

## Leaf Buds & Twigs

Bud Type: ○ Terminal (grows at tip of a shoot causing shoot to grow longer)
○ Lateral (grow along sides of a shoot causing sideways growth)

Twig Features: ○ Smooth  ○ Hairy  ○ Spines  ○ Corky Ribs
○ (Other) _____

Notes: _____

## Bark

Texture: ○ Furrowed  ○ Scaly  ○ Peeling  ○ Smooth  ○ Shiny
○ Fissured  ○ Ridges / Depressions  ○ Papery  ○ Warty
○ (Other) _____

Color: ○ Gray  ○ Brown  ○ Cinnamon  ○ White  ○ Silver
○ Green  ○ Copper  ○ (Other) _____

Notes: _____

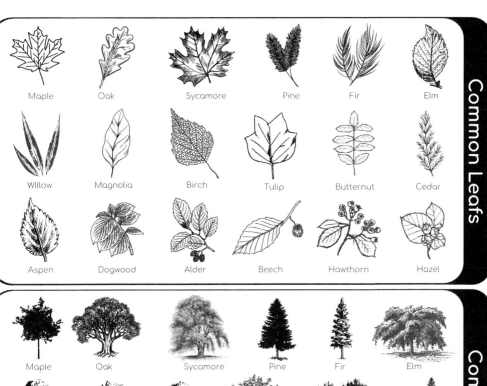

Maple    Oak    Sycamore    Pine    Fir    Elm

Willow    Magnolia    Birch    Tulip    Butternut    Cedar

Aspen    Dogwood    Alder    Beech    Hawthorn    Hazel

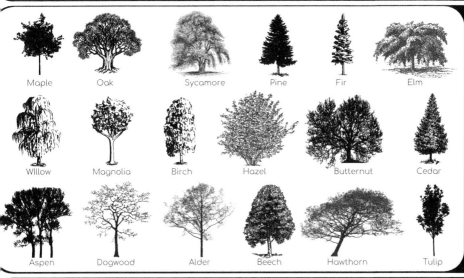

Maple    Oak    Sycamore    Pine    Fir    Elm

Willow    Magnolia    Birch    Hazel    Butternut    Cedar

Aspen    Dogwood    Alder    Beech    Hawthorn    Tulip

## Environment

Location / GPS: _____ Date _____

Season: ○ Spring ○ Summer ○ Fall ○ Winter

Surroundings: ○ Hedgerows ○ Field ○ Park ○ Woodland ○ Water
○ Other _____

Setting: ○ Natural ○ Artificial     Type: ○ Evergreen ○ Deciduous

Notes: _____
_____
_____

## General

Shape: ○ Vase ○ Columnar ○ Round ○ (Other) _____

Features: ○ Conical/Spire ○ Spreading ○ Upright ○ Weeping
○ (Other) _____

Branching: ○ Opposite ○ Alternate     Estimated Age: _____

Notes: _____
_____
_____

## Needles or Leaves

Type: ○ Needle ○ Simple Broadleaf ○ Compound Broadleaf ○ Scales

Shape: ○ Cordate (heart-shaped) ○ Lanceolate (long and narrow)
○ Deltoid (triangular) ○ Obicular (round) ○ Ovate (egg-shaped)
○ Palm and Maple ○ Lobed

Structure: ○ Simple (attached to twigs or twig stems)
○ Compound (attached to single lead steam)

Notes: _____
_____
_____

## Flowers, Fruits & Seeds

Flower Type: ○ Single Blooms ○ Clustered Blooms ○ Catkins

Fruits / Seeds: ○ Berries ○ Apples ○ Pears ○ Nuts ○ Acorns
○ Cones ○ Capsules ○ Catkins ○ (Other) _____

Notes: _____
_____
_____

## Leaf Buds & Twigs

Bud Type: ○ Terminal (grows at tip of a shoot causing shoot to grow longer)
○ Lateral (grow along sides of a shoot causing sideways growth)

Twig Features: ○ Smooth ○ Hairy ○ Spines ○ Corky Ribs
○ (Other) _____

Notes: _____

## Bark

Texture: ○ Furrowed ○ Scaly ○ Peeling ○ Smooth ○ Shiny
○ Fissured ○ Ridges / Depressions ○ Papery ○ Warty
○ (Other) _____

Color: ○ Gray ○ Brown ○ Cinnamon ○ White ○ Silver
○ Green ○ Copper ○ (Other) _____

Notes: _____

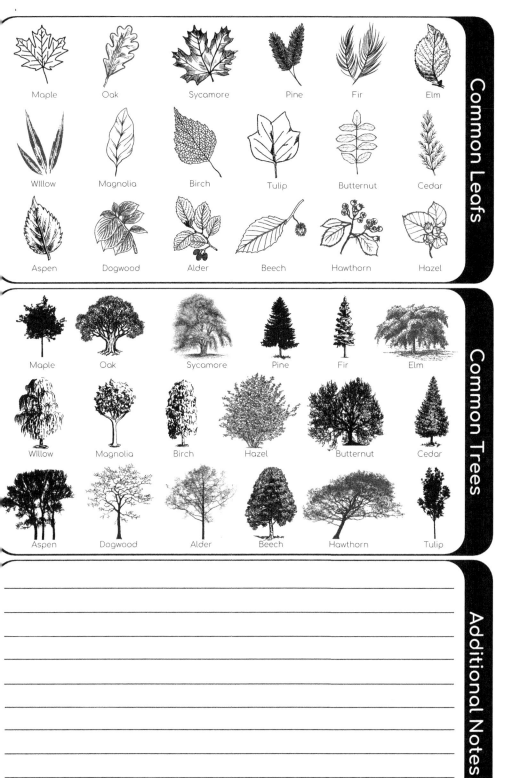

Maple    Oak    Sycamore    Pine    Fir    Elm

WIllow    Magnolia    Birch    Tulip    Butternut    Cedar

Aspen    Dogwood    Alder    Beech    Hawthorn    Hazel

Maple    Oak    Sycamore    Pine    Fir    Elm

WIllow    Magnolia    Birch    Hazel    Butternut    Cedar

Aspen    Dogwood    Alder    Beech    Hawthorn    Tulip

## Environment

Location / GPS: _____ Date _____

Season: ○ Spring ○ Summer ○ Fall ○ Winter

Surroundings: ○ Hedgerows ○ Field ○ Park ○ Woodland ○ Water
○ Other _____

Setting: ○ Natural ○ Artificial   Type: ○ Evergreen ○ Deciduous

Notes: _____
_____

## General

Shape: ○ Vase ○ Columnar ○ Round ○ (Other) _____

Features: ○ Conical/Spire ○ Spreading ○ Upright ○ Weeping
○ (Other) _____

Branching: ○ Opposite ○ Alternate   Estimated Age: _____

Notes: _____
_____

## Needles or Leaves

Type: ○ Needle ○ Simple Broadleaf ○ Compound Broadleaf ○ Scales

Shape: ○ Cordate (heart-shaped) ○ Lanceolate (long and narrow)
○ Deltoid (triangular) ○ Obicular (round) ○ Ovate (egg-shaped)
○ Palm and Maple ○ Lobed

Structure: ○ Simple (attached to twigs or twig stems)
○ Compound (attached to single lead steam)

Notes: _____
_____

## Flowers, Fruits & Seeds

Flower Type: ○ Single Blooms ○ Clustered Blooms ○ Catkins

Fruits / Seeds: ○ Berries ○ Apples ○ Pears ○ Nuts ○ Acorns
○ Cones ○ Capsules ○ Catkins ○ (Other) _____

Notes: _____
_____

## Leaf Buds & Twigs

Bud Type: ○ Terminal (grows at tip of a shoot causing shoot to grow longer)
○ Lateral (grow along sides of a shoot causing sideways growth)

Twig Features: ○ Smooth ○ Hairy ○ Spines ○ Corky Ribs
○ (Other) _____

Notes: _____

## Bark

Texture: ○ Furrowed ○ Scaly ○ Peeling ○ Smooth ○ Shiny
○ Fissured ○ Ridges / Depressions ○ Papery ○ Warty
○ (Other) _____

Color: ○ Gray ○ Brown ○ Cinnamon ○ White ○ Silver
○ Green ○ Copper ○ (Other) _____

Notes: _____

Maple    Oak    Sycamore    Pine    Fir    Elm

Wlllow    Magnolia    Birch    Tulip    Butternut    Cedar

Aspen    Dogwood    Alder    Beech    Hawthorn    Hazel

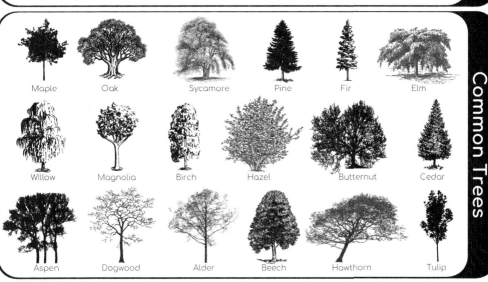

Maple    Oak    Sycamore    Pine    Fir    Elm

Wlllow    Magnolia    Birch    Hazel    Butternut    Cedar

Aspen    Dogwood    Alder    Beech    Hawthorn    Tulip

## Environment

Location / GPS: _____ Date _____

Season: ○ Spring ○ Summer ○ Fall ○ Winter

Surroundings: ○ Hedgerows ○ Field ○ Park ○ Woodland ○ Water
○ Other _____

Setting: ○ Natural ○ Artificial **Type:** ○ Evergreen ○ Deciduous

Notes: _____
_____

## General

Shape: ○ Vase ○ Columnar ○ Round ○ (Other) _____

Features: ○ Conical/Spire ○ Spreading ○ Upright ○ Weeping
○ (Other) _____

Branching: ○ Opposite ○ Alternate **Estimated Age:** _____

Notes: _____
_____

## Needles or Leaves

Type: ○ Needle ○ Simple Broadleaf ○ Compound Broadleaf ○ Scales

Shape: ○ Cordate (heart-shaped) ○ Lanceolate (long and narrow)
○ Deltoid (triangular) ○ Obicular (round) ○ Ovate (egg-shaped)
○ Palm and Maple ○ Lobed

Structure: ○ Simple (attached to twigs or twig stems)
○ Compound (attached to single lead steam)

Notes: _____
_____

## Flowers, Fruits & Seeds

Flower Type: ○ Single Blooms ○ Clustered Blooms ○ Catkins

Fruits / Seeds: ○ Berries ○ Apples ○ Pears ○ Nuts ○ Acorns
○ Cones ○ Capsules ○ Catkins ○ (Other) _____

Notes: _____
_____

## Leaf Buds & Twigs

Bud Type: ○ Terminal (grows at tip of a shoot causing shoot to grow longer)
○ Lateral (grow along sides of a shoot causing sideways growth)

Twig Features: ○ Smooth ○ Hairy ○ Spines ○ Corky Ribs
○ (Other) _____

Notes: _____

## Bark

Texture: ○ Furrowed ○ Scaly ○ Peeling ○ Smooth ○ Shiny
○ Fissured ○ Ridges / Depressions ○ Papery ○ Warty
○ (Other) _____

Color: ○ Gray ○ Brown ○ Cinnamon ○ White ○ Silver
○ Green ○ Copper ○ (Other) _____

Notes: _____

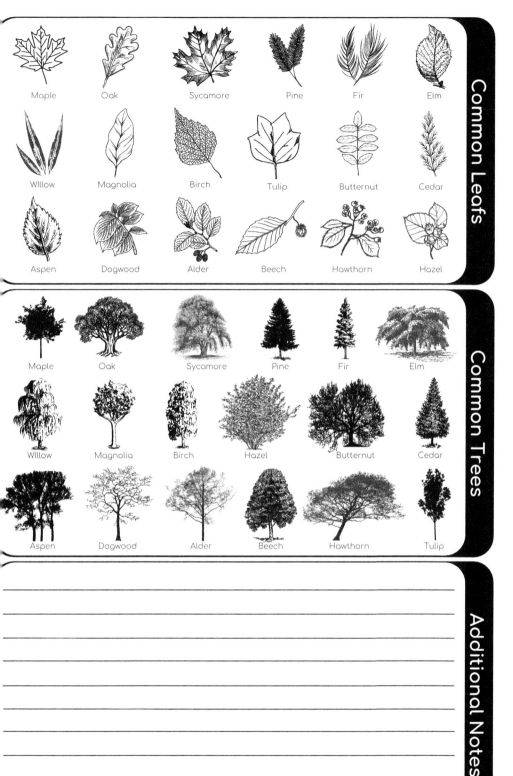

Maple    Oak    Sycamore    Pine    Fir    Elm

WIllow    Magnolia    Birch    Tulip    Butternut    Cedar

Aspen    Dogwood    Alder    Beech    Hawthorn    Hazel

Maple    Oak    Sycamore    Pine    Fir    Elm

WIllow    Magnolia    Birch    Hazel    Butternut    Cedar

Aspen    Dogwood    Alder    Beech    Hawthorn    Tulip

## Environment

Location / GPS: _____  Date _____

Season: ○ Spring  ○ Summer  ○ Fall  ○ Winter

Surroundings: ○ Hedgerows  ○ Field  ○ Park  ○ Woodland  ○ Water
○ Other _____

Setting: ○ Natural  ○ Artificial   **Type:** ○ Evergreen  ○ Deciduous

Notes: _____
_____
_____

## General

Shape: ○ Vase  ○ Columnar  ○ Round  ○ (Other) _____

Features: ○ Conical/Spire  ○ Spreading  ○ Upright  ○ Weeping
○ (Other) _____

Branching: ○ Opposite  ○ Alternate   **Estimated Age:** _____

Notes: _____
_____

## Needles or Leaves

Type: ○ Needle  ○ Simple Broadleaf  ○ Compound Broadleaf  ○ Scales

Shape: ○ Cordate (heart-shaped)  ○ Lanceolate (long and narrow)
○ Deltoid (triangular)  ○ Obicular (round)  ○ Ovate (egg-shaped)
○ Palm and Maple  ○ Lobed

Structure: ○ Simple (attached to twigs or twig stems)
○ Compound (attached to single lead steam)

Notes: _____
_____
_____

## Flowers, Fruits & Seeds

Flower Type: ○ Single Blooms  ○ Clustered Blooms  ○ Catkins

Fruits / Seeds: ○ Berries  ○ Apples  ○ Pears  ○ Nuts  ○ Acorns
○ Cones  ○ Capsules  ○ Catkins  ○ (Other) _____

Notes: _____
_____
_____

## Leaf Buds & Twigs

Bud Type: ○ Terminal (grows at tip of a shoot causing shoot to grow longer)
○ Lateral (grow along sides of a shoot causing sideways growth)

Twig Features: ○ Smooth  ○ Hairy  ○ Spines  ○ Corky Ribs
○ (Other) _____

Notes: _____
_____

## Bark

Texture: ○ Furrowed  ○ Scaly  ○ Peeling  ○ Smooth  ○ Shiny
○ Fissured  ○ Ridges / Depressions  ○ Papery  ○ Warty
○ (Other) _____

Color: ○ Gray  ○ Brown  ○ Cinnamon  ○ White  ○ Silver
○ Green  ○ Copper  ○ (Other) _____

Notes: _____

Maple  Oak  Sycamore  Pine  Fir  Elm

Willow  Magnolia  Birch  Tulip  Butternut  Cedar

Aspen  Dogwood  Alder  Beech  Hawthorn  Hazel

Maple  Oak  Sycamore  Pine  Fir  Elm

Willow  Magnolia  Birch  Hazel  Butternut  Cedar

Aspen  Dogwood  Alder  Beech  Hawthorn  Tulip

## Environment

Location / GPS: _____ Date _____

Season: ○ Spring ○ Summer ○ Fall ○ Winter

Surroundings: ○ Hedgerows ○ Field ○ Park ○ Woodland ○ Water
○ Other _____

Setting: ○ Natural ○ Artificial   Type: ○ Evergreen ○ Deciduous

Notes: _____
_____
_____

## General

Shape: ○ Vase ○ Columnar ○ Round ○ (Other) _____

Features: ○ Conical/Spire ○ Spreading ○ Upright ○ Weeping
○ (Other) _____

Branching: ○ Opposite ○ Alternate   Estimated Age: _____

Notes: _____
_____
_____

## Needles or Leaves

Type: ○ Needle ○ Simple Broadleaf ○ Compound Broadleaf ○ Scales

Shape: ○ Cordate (heart-shaped) ○ Lanceolate (long and narrow)
○ Deltoid (triangular) ○ Obicular (round) ○ Ovate (egg-shaped)
○ Palm and Maple ○ Lobed

Structure: ○ Simple (attached to twigs or twig stems)
○ Compound (attached to single lead steam)

Notes: _____
_____
_____

## Flowers, Fruits & Seeds

Flower Type: ○ Single Blooms ○ Clustered Blooms ○ Catkins

Fruits / Seeds: ○ Berries ○ Apples ○ Pears ○ Nuts ○ Acorns
○ Cones ○ Capsules ○ Catkins ○ (Other) _____

Notes: _____
_____
_____

## Leaf Buds & Twigs

Bud Type: ○ Terminal (grows at tip of a shoot causing shoot to grow longer)
○ Lateral (grow along sides of a shoot causing sideways growth)

Twig Features: ○ Smooth ○ Hairy ○ Spines ○ Corky Ribs
○ (Other) _____

Notes: _____
_____

## Bark

Texture: ○ Furrowed ○ Scaly ○ Peeling ○ Smooth ○ Shiny
○ Fissured ○ Ridges / Depressions ○ Papery ○ Warty
○ (Other) _____

Color: ○ Gray ○ Brown ○ Cinnamon ○ White ○ Silver
○ Green ○ Copper ○ (Other) _____

Notes: _____

Maple  Oak  Sycamore  Pine  Fir  Elm

Wlllow  Magnolia  Birch  Tulip  Butternut  Cedar

Aspen  Dogwood  Alder  Beech  Hawthorn  Hazel

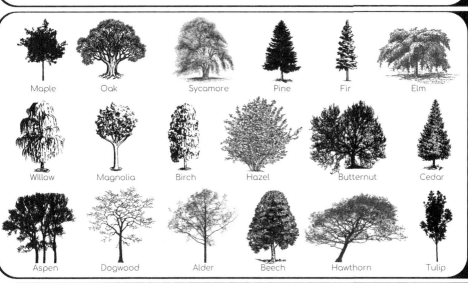

Maple  Oak  Sycamore  Pine  Fir  Elm

Wlllow  Magnolia  Birch  Hazel  Butternut  Cedar

Aspen  Dogwood  Alder  Beech  Hawthorn  Tulip

## Environment

Location / GPS: _____ Date _____

Season: ◯ Spring  ◯ Summer  ◯ Fall  ◯ Winter

Surroundings: ◯ Hedgerows  ◯ Field  ◯ Park  ◯ Woodland  ◯ Water
◯ Other_____

Setting: ◯ Natural  ◯ Artificial     Type: ◯ Evergreen  ◯ Deciduous

Notes: _____
_____

## General

Shape: ◯ Vase  ◯ Columnar  ◯ Round  ◯ (Other) _____

Features: ◯ Conical/Spire  ◯ Spreading  ◯ Upright  ◯ Weeping
◯ (Other) _____

Branching: ◯ Opposite  ◯ Alternate     Estimated Age: _____

Notes: _____
_____

## Needles or Leaves

Type: ◯ Needle  ◯ Simple Broadleaf  ◯ Compound Broadleaf  ◯ Scales

Shape: ◯ Cordate (heart-shaped)  ◯ Lanceolate (long and narrow)
◯ Deltoid (triangular)  ◯ Obicular (round)  ◯ Ovate (egg-shaped)
◯ Palm and Maple  ◯ Lobed

Structure: ◯ Simple (attached to twigs or twig stems)
◯ Compound (attached to single lead steam)

Notes: _____
_____

## Flowers, Fruits & Seeds

Flower Type: ◯ Single Blooms  ◯ Clustered Blooms  ◯ Catkins

Fruits / Seeds: ◯ Berries  ◯ Apples  ◯ Pears  ◯ Nuts  ◯ Acorns
◯ Cones  ◯ Capsules  ◯ Catkins  ◯ (Other) _____

Notes: _____
_____

## Leaf Buds & Twigs

Bud Type: ◯ Terminal (grows at tip of a shoot causing shoot to grow longer)
◯ Lateral (grow along sides of a shoot causing sideways growth)

Twig Features: ◯ Smooth  ◯ Hairy  ◯ Spines  ◯ Corky Ribs
◯ (Other) _____

Notes: _____

## Bark

Texture: ◯ Furrowed  ◯ Scaly  ◯ Peeling  ◯ Smooth  ◯ Shiny
◯ Fissured  ◯ Ridges / Depressions  ◯ Papery  ◯ Warty
◯ (Other) _____

Color: ◯ Gray  ◯ Brown  ◯ Cinnamon  ◯ White  ◯ Silver
◯ Green  ◯ Copper  ◯ (Other) _____

Notes: _____

Maple    Oak    Sycamore    Pine    Fir    Elm

WIllow    Magnolia    Birch    Tulip    Butternut    Cedar

Aspen    Dogwood    Alder    Beech    Hawthorn    Hazel

Maple    Oak    Sycamore    Pine    Fir    Elm

WIllow    Magnolia    Birch    Hazel    Butternut    Cedar

Aspen    Dogwood    Alder    Beech    Hawthorn    Tulip

## Environment

Location / GPS: _____ Date _____

Season: ○ Spring ○ Summer ○ Fall ○ Winter

Surroundings: ○ Hedgerows ○ Field ○ Park ○ Woodland ○ Water
○ Other _____

Setting: ○ Natural ○ Artificial     Type: ○ Evergreen ○ Deciduous

Notes: _____
_____
_____

## General

Shape: ○ Vase ○ Columnar ○ Round ○ (Other) _____

Features: ○ Conical/Spire ○ Spreading ○ Upright ○ Weeping
○ (Other) _____

Branching: ○ Opposite ○ Alternate     Estimated Age: _____

Notes: _____
_____
_____

## Needles or Leaves

Type: ○ Needle ○ Simple Broadleaf ○ Compound Broadleaf ○ Scales

Shape: ○ Cordate (heart-shaped) ○ Lanceolate (long and narrow)
○ Deltoid (triangular) ○ Obicular (round) ○ Ovate (egg-shaped)
○ Palm and Maple ○ Lobed

Structure: ○ Simple (attached to twigs or twig stems)
○ Compound (attached to single lead steam)

Notes: _____
_____
_____

## Flowers, Fruits & Seeds

Flower Type: ○ Single Blooms ○ Clustered Blooms ○ Catkins

Fruits / Seeds: ○ Berries ○ Apples ○ Pears ○ Nuts ○ Acorns
○ Cones ○ Capsules ○ Catkins ○ (Other) _____

Notes: _____
_____
_____

## Leaf Buds & Twigs

Bud Type: ○ Terminal (grows at tip of a shoot causing shoot to grow longer)
○ Lateral (grow along sides of a shoot causing sideways growth)

Twig Features: ○ Smooth ○ Hairy ○ Spines ○ Corky Ribs
○ (Other) _____

Notes: _____

## Bark

Texture: ○ Furrowed ○ Scaly ○ Peeling ○ Smooth ○ Shiny
○ Fissured ○ Ridges / Depressions ○ Papery ○ Warty
○ (Other) _____

Color: ○ Gray ○ Brown ○ Cinnamon ○ White ○ Silver
○ Green ○ Copper ○ (Other) _____

Notes: _____

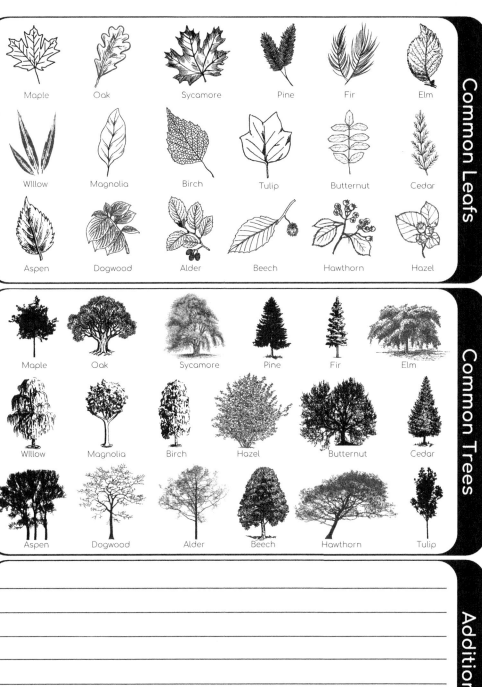

Maple    Oak    Sycamore    Pine    Fir    Elm

Wlllow    Magnolia    Birch    Tulip    Butternut    Cedar

Aspen    Dogwood    Alder    Beech    Hawthorn    Hazel

Maple    Oak    Sycamore    Pine    Fir    Elm

Wlllow    Magnolia    Birch    Hazel    Butternut    Cedar

Aspen    Dogwood    Alder    Beech    Hawthorn    Tulip

## Environment

Location / GPS: _____ Date _____

Season: ○ Spring  ○ Summer  ○ Fall  ○ Winter

Surroundings: ○ Hedgerows  ○ Field  ○ Park  ○ Woodland  ○ Water
○ Other _____

Setting: ○ Natural  ○ Artificial  **Type:** ○ Evergreen  ○ Deciduous

Notes: _____
_____
_____

## General

Shape: ○ Vase  ○ Columnar  ○ Round  ○ (Other) _____

Features: ○ Conical/Spire  ○ Spreading  ○ Upright  ○ Weeping
○ (Other) _____

Branching: ○ Opposite  ○ Alternate  **Estimated Age:** _____

Notes: _____
_____

## Needles or Leaves

Type: ○ Needle  ○ Simple Broadleaf  ○ Compound Broadleaf  ○ Scales

Shape: ○ Cordate (heart-shaped)  ○ Lanceolate (long and narrow)
○ Deltoid (triangular)  ○ Obicular (round)  ○ Ovate (egg-shaped)
○ Palm and Maple  ○ Lobed

Structure: ○ Simple (attached to twigs or twig stems)
○ Compound (attached to single lead steam)

Notes: _____
_____

## Flowers, Fruits & Seeds

Flower Type: ○ Single Blooms  ○ Clustered Blooms  ○ Catkins

Fruits / Seeds: ○ Berries  ○ Apples  ○ Pears  ○ Nuts  ○ Acorns
○ Cones  ○ Capsules  ○ Catkins  ○ (Other) _____

Notes: _____
_____

## Leaf Buds & Twigs

Bud Type: ○ Terminal (grows at tip of a shoot causing shoot to grow longer)
○ Lateral (grow along sides of a shoot causing sideways growth)

Twig Features: ○ Smooth  ○ Hairy  ○ Spines  ○ Corky Ribs
○ (Other) _____

Notes: _____

## Bark

Texture: ○ Furrowed  ○ Scaly  ○ Peeling  ○ Smooth  ○ Shiny
○ Fissured  ○ Ridges / Depressions  ○ Papery  ○ Warty
○ (Other) _____

Color: ○ Gray  ○ Brown  ○ Cinnamon  ○ White  ○ Silver
○ Green  ○ Copper  ○ (Other) _____

Notes: _____

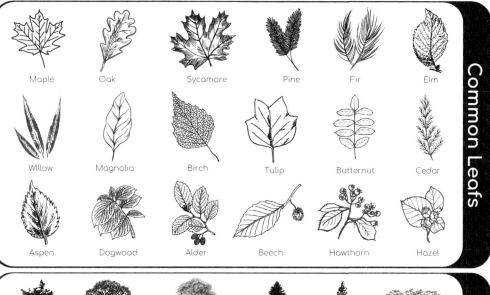

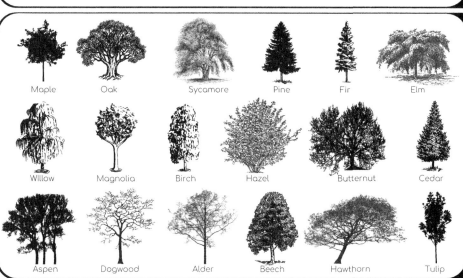

## Environment

Location / GPS: _____ Date _____

Season: ○ Spring ○ Summer ○ Fall ○ Winter

Surroundings: ○ Hedgerows ○ Field ○ Park ○ Woodland ○ Water
○ Other _____

Setting: ○ Natural ○ Artificial    Type: ○ Evergreen ○ Deciduous

Notes: _____
_____

## General

Shape: ○ Vase ○ Columnar ○ Round ○ (Other) _____

Features: ○ Conical/Spire ○ Spreading ○ Upright ○ Weeping
○ (Other) _____

Branching: ○ Opposite ○ Alternate    Estimated Age: _____

Notes: _____
_____

## Needles or Leaves

Type: ○ Needle ○ Simple Broadleaf ○ Compound Broadleaf ○ Scales

Shape: ○ Cordate (heart-shaped) ○ Lanceolate (long and narrow)
○ Deltoid (triangular) ○ Obicular (round) ○ Ovate (egg-shaped)
○ Palm and Maple ○ Lobed

Structure: ○ Simple (attached to twigs or twig stems)
○ Compound (attached to single lead steam)

Notes: _____
_____

## Flowers, Fruits & Seeds

Flower Type: ○ Single Blooms ○ Clustered Blooms ○ Catkins

Fruits / Seeds: ○ Berries ○ Apples ○ Pears ○ Nuts ○ Acorns
○ Cones ○ Capsules ○ Catkins ○ (Other) _____

Notes: _____
_____

## Leaf Buds & Twigs

Bud Type: ○ Terminal (grows at tip of a shoot causing shoot to grow longer)
○ Lateral (grow along sides of a shoot causing sideways growth)

Twig Features: ○ Smooth ○ Hairy ○ Spines ○ Corky Ribs
○ (Other) _____

Notes: _____

## Bark

Texture: ○ Furrowed ○ Scaly ○ Peeling ○ Smooth ○ Shiny
○ Fissured ○ Ridges / Depressions ○ Papery ○ Warty
○ (Other) _____

Color: ○ Gray ○ Brown ○ Cinnamon ○ White ○ Silver
○ Green ○ Copper ○ (Other) _____

Notes: _____

Maple
Oak
Sycamore
Pine
Fir
Elm

WIllow
Magnolia
Birch
Tulip
Butternut
Cedar

Aspen
Dogwood
Alder
Beech
Hawthorn
Hazel

Maple
Oak
Sycamore
Pine
Fir
Elm

WIllow
Magnolia
Birch
Hazel
Butternut
Cedar

Aspen
Dogwood
Alder
Beech
Hawthorn
Tulip

## Environment

Location / GPS: _____ Date _____

Season: ○ Spring ○ Summer ○ Fall ○ Winter

Surroundings: ○ Hedgerows ○ Field ○ Park ○ Woodland ○ Water
○ Other _____

Setting: ○ Natural ○ Artificial Type: ○ Evergreen ○ Deciduous

Notes: _____
_____
_____

## General

Shape: ○ Vase ○ Columnar ○ Round ○ (Other) _____

Features: ○ Conical/Spire ○ Spreading ○ Upright ○ Weeping
○ (Other) _____

Branching: ○ Opposite ○ Alternate Estimated Age: _____

Notes: _____
_____
_____

## Needles or Leaves

Type: ○ Needle ○ Simple Broadleaf ○ Compound Broadleaf ○ Scales

Shape: ○ Cordate (heart-shaped) ○ Lanceolate (long and narrow)
○ Deltoid (triangular) ○ Obicular (round) ○ Ovate (egg-shaped)
○ Palm and Maple ○ Lobed

Structure: ○ Simple (attached to twigs or twig stems)
○ Compound (attached to single lead steam)

Notes: _____
_____
_____

## Flowers, Fruits & Seeds

Flower Type: ○ Single Blooms ○ Clustered Blooms ○ Catkins

Fruits / Seeds: ○ Berries ○ Apples ○ Pears ○ Nuts ○ Acorns
○ Cones ○ Capsules ○ Catkins ○ (Other) _____

Notes: _____
_____
_____

## Leaf Buds & Twigs

Bud Type: ○ Terminal (grows at tip of a shoot causing shoot to grow longer)
○ Lateral (grow along sides of a shoot causing sideways growth)

Twig Features: ○ Smooth ○ Hairy ○ Spines ○ Corky Ribs
○ (Other) _____

Notes: _____

## Bark

Texture: ○ Furrowed ○ Scaly ○ Peeling ○ Smooth ○ Shiny
○ Fissured ○ Ridges / Depressions ○ Papery ○ Warty
○ (Other) _____

Color: ○ Gray ○ Brown ○ Cinnamon ○ White ○ Silver
○ Green ○ Copper ○ (Other) _____

Notes: _____

## Environment

Location / GPS: _____ Date _____

Season: ○ Spring ○ Summer ○ Fall ○ Winter

Surroundings: ○ Hedgerows ○ Field ○ Park ○ Woodland ○ Water
○ Other _____

Setting: ○ Natural ○ Artificial   Type: ○ Evergreen ○ Deciduous

Notes: _____
_____

## General

Shape: ○ Vase ○ Columnar ○ Round ○ (Other) _____

Features: ○ Conical/Spire ○ Spreading ○ Upright ○ Weeping
○ (Other) _____

Branching: ○ Opposite ○ Alternate   Estimated Age: _____

Notes: _____
_____

## Needles or Leaves

Type: ○ Needle ○ Simple Broadleaf ○ Compound Broadleaf ○ Scales

Shape: ○ Cordate (heart-shaped) ○ Lanceolate (long and narrow)
○ Deltoid (triangular) ○ Obicular (round) ○ Ovate (egg-shaped)
○ Palm and Maple ○ Lobed

Structure: ○ Simple (attached to twigs or twig stems)
○ Compound (attached to single lead steam)

Notes: _____
_____

## Flowers, Fruits & Seeds

Flower Type: ○ Single Blooms ○ Clustered Blooms ○ Catkins

Fruits / Seeds: ○ Berries ○ Apples ○ Pears ○ Nuts ○ Acorns
○ Cones ○ Capsules ○ Catkins ○ (Other) _____

Notes: _____
_____

## Leaf Buds & Twigs

Bud Type: ○ Terminal (grows at tip of a shoot causing shoot to grow longer)
○ Lateral (grow along sides of a shoot causing sideways growth)

Twig Features: ○ Smooth ○ Hairy ○ Spines ○ Corky Ribs
○ (Other) _____

Notes: _____

## Bark

Texture: ○ Furrowed ○ Scaly ○ Peeling ○ Smooth ○ Shiny
○ Fissured ○ Ridges / Depressions ○ Papery ○ Warty
○ (Other) _____

Color: ○ Gray ○ Brown ○ Cinnamon ○ White ○ Silver
○ Green ○ Copper ○ (Other) _____

Notes: _____

Maple    Oak    Sycamore    Pine    Fir    Elm

WIllow    Magnolia    Birch    Tulip    Butternut    Cedar

Aspen    Dogwood    Alder    Beech    Hawthorn    Hazel

Maple    Oak    Sycamore    Pine    Fir    Elm

WIllow    Magnolia    Birch    Hazel    Butternut    Cedar

Aspen    Dogwood    Alder    Beech    Hawthorn    Tulip

## Environment

Location / GPS: _____ Date _____

Season: ◯ Spring  ◯ Summer  ◯ Fall  ◯ Winter

Surroundings: ◯ Hedgerows  ◯ Field  ◯ Park  ◯ Woodland  ◯ Water
◯ Other _____

Setting: ◯ Natural  ◯ Artificial  **Type:** ◯ Evergreen  ◯ Deciduous

Notes: _____
_____

## General

Shape: ◯ Vase  ◯ Columnar  ◯ Round  ◯ (Other) _____

Features: ◯ Conical/Spire  ◯ Spreading  ◯ Upright  ◯ Weeping
◯ (Other) _____

Branching: ◯ Opposite  ◯ Alternate  **Estimated Age:** _____

Notes: _____
_____

## Needles or Leaves

Type: ◯ Needle  ◯ Simple Broadleaf  ◯ Compound Broadleaf  ◯ Scales

Shape: ◯ Cordate (heart-shaped)  ◯ Lanceolate (long and narrow)
◯ Deltoid (triangular)  ◯ Obicular (round)  ◯ Ovate (egg-shaped)
◯ Palm and Maple  ◯ Lobed

Structure: ◯ Simple (attached to twigs or twig stems)
◯ Compound (attached to single lead steam)

Notes: _____
_____

## Flowers, Fruits & Seeds

Flower Type: ◯ Single Blooms  ◯ Clustered Blooms  ◯ Catkins

Fruits / Seeds: ◯ Berries ◯ Apples ◯ Pears ◯ Nuts ◯ Acorns
◯ Cones  ◯ Capsules  ◯ Catkins  ◯ (Other) _____

Notes: _____
_____

## Leaf Buds & Twigs

Bud Type: ◯ Terminal (grows at tip of a shoot causing shoot to grow longer)
◯ Lateral (grow along sides of a shoot causing sideways growth)

Twig Features: ◯ Smooth ◯ Hairy  ◯ Spines  ◯ Corky Ribs
◯ (Other) _____

Notes: _____

## Bark

Texture: ◯ Furrowed ◯ Scaly ◯ Peeling ◯ Smooth ◯ Shiny
◯ Fissured ◯ Ridges / Depressions ◯ Papery ◯ Warty
◯ (Other) _____

Color: ◯ Gray ◯ Brown ◯ Cinnamon ◯ White ◯ Silver
◯ Green ◯ Copper ◯ (Other) _____

Notes: _____

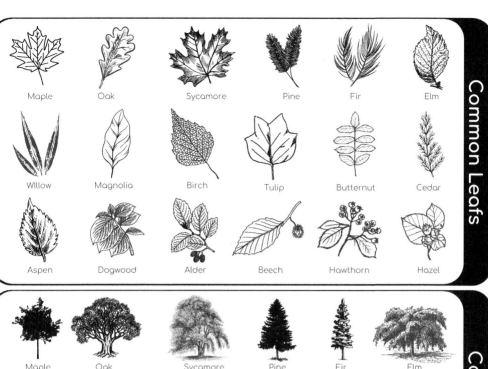

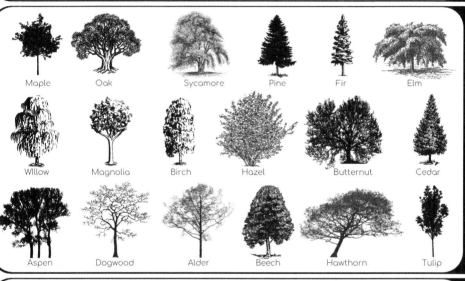

Printed in Great Britain
by Amazon

81869827R00068